GOLF IS A WOMAN'S GAME

Jane Horn

Adams Media Corporation

HOLBROOK, MASSACHUSETTS

To my mother,
without her encouragement this book
would not have been possible.

• •

Published by
Adams Media Corporation
260 Center Street, Holbrook, MA 02343

ISBN: 1-55850-711-6

Printed in Canada.

J H G F E D C B A

Library of Congress Cataloging-in-Publication Data
Horn, Jane (Jane G.)
Golf is a woman's game / Jane Horn. — 1st ed.
p.   cm.
ISBN 1-55850-711-6
1. Golf for women. I. Title.
GV966.H67   1997
796.352'082—dc21   97-7905
                                          CIP

Front cover image ©Focus on Sports, Inc.
Rear cover image ©Index Stock Photography
Interior illustrations by Bob Brangwynne

This publication is designed to provide accurate and authoritative information with regard to the subject matter covered. It is sold with the understanding that the publisher is not engaged in rendering legal, accounting, or other professional advice. If legal advice or other expert assistance is required, the services of a competent professional person should be sought.
—From a *Declaration of Principles* jointly adopted by a Committee of the American Bar Association and a Committee of Publishers and Associations

This book is available at quantity discounts for bulk purchases.
For information, call 1-800-872-5627 (in Massachusetts, 617-767-8100).

Visit our home page at http://www.adamsmedia.com

CH 10/97

Contents

Introduction

For many years golf has been viewed as a man's game. Even the word *golf* is said to be an acronym for "Gentlemen Only; Ladies Forbidden." When a woman steps onto a golf course, she is often made to feel like an unwanted guest treading on male territory. The truth is, golf is a woman's game as well. Although many men would like to think that they are naturally superior when it comes to golf, this book contends that women have a natural ability for golf that surpasses that of their male counterparts.

Male bias in golf is not restricted to the golf course. It is also found in golf instruction. Golf pros perpetuate many myths about women's golf swings, which have hindered talented women from achieving their golfing potential.

The intention of my book is to dismiss all the misinformation given to women regarding their golf swings. Throughout this book I have discussed common golfing myths. I am more than certain that each of you has heard at least one, if not all, of these myths during your golfing career.

In reading this book most of you will find that what you have been taught about what makes a good golf swing is incorrect. Many of you may have spent years trying to implement these erroneous instructions. Well, take heart because in this book you will find correct information and simple instructions that, if followed properly, I guarantee will improve your game.

— *Jane Horn*

1

The Address

Before hitting the ball, you should assume a position from which you will execute your swing. This position is commonly referred to as the address, or setup. The address should consist of a proper stance, posture, grip, and alignment. The manner in which you set yourself up to the ball is crucial for the execution of a good shot.

In addressing the ball, ideally the arms should be hanging as vertically as possible to the ground. This means that both arms will be straight, but gravity, not tension, should create their straightness. You simply want to bend from the hips and allow the arms to hang in a relaxed but straight position. Think of allowing your arms and the shaft of the club to form the letter Y. This Y will be a very relaxed Y, in which you will tilt at the stem of the Y about forty-five degrees perpendicular to the Y itself. The reason we want the stem of the Y to be tilted at forty-five degrees is that, as you will

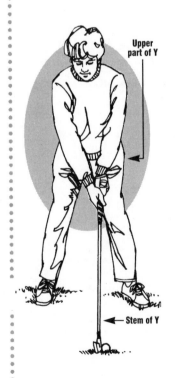

Upper part of Y

Stem of Y

Front view of the address.

notice in the illustration, this puts the hands in a precocked position. This will be important in allowing you to swing the club back correctly (see Chapter 3 on the backswing).

Your feet should be about shoulder-width apart, with the toes of the feet pointing slightly outward. We create this position solely for establishing balance.

You should distribute your weight equally between the left and right feet, with the knees slightly flexed. This is a "ready" position: legs flexed but not bent, and feet well in balance but prepared to move in any direction. When you assume your ready position, be sure your weight is not on your heels or toes, but rather on the balls of your feet. Good balance is essential to a golf swing, so make sure you are in balance at your address.

Your head should be positioned slightly to the right of the ball. You must be aware of what you do with your head, as it provides two functions in the golf swing: it is where your visual center is located, and it is where your weight will be. Do not get the two confused. You want to see the ball, but not by hanging over it because this will put your body out of balance on the backswing. You simply want to look near the ball and allow the head to assume its normal posture. It is extremely important to bend from the hips and not the waist. You need to bend over to reach the ball, but the trick is knowing how to bend. You are setting a posture for your golf swing that is going to establish your angled relationship to the ball.

This is why you should use your hips as your bending point. By tilting from your hips, the spinal column stays relatively straight, enabling you to keep your posture throughout the swing.

The ball should be positioned between the feet, left of the center for the irons, and off the left heel for the woods. The distance you should stand from the ball can be measured by placing the little finger of the left hand on your front left thigh. Once your hand is in place,

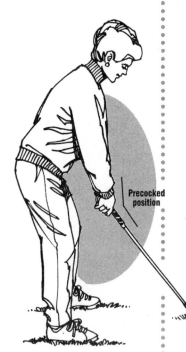

Precocked position

Notice the 45 degree angle that is created by the shaft of the club and the arms. It is this angle that sets the hand in a precocked position.

spread the fingers apart. This is the approximate distance the hands and the club handle should be from your body with all clubs. With the longer clubs, you simply adjust by moving farther away from the ball. And, of course, with shorter clubs, you will move closer. Either way, the hand and handle position should be the same. You will notice at this distance the arms will be hanging vertically, and the wrists will have assumed the desired precocked position.

Every movement in the golf swing should help maintain the right angle formed by the cocked wrists (see Chapter 3 on the backswing), and when the ball is played toward the right foot, it promotes an early release of this angle. When the ball is placed left of the center, the hands can maintain their angle longer. With the woods, the ball should be placed off the left heel. You are trying to hit the ball not at the bottom of the swing's arc, but rather after the swing has reached the bottom and is returning up—in other words, on the upswing. Be careful when you position the ball between your feet because it is not just the position of the ball relative to your feet that is important; it is also the ball's position to the upper body.

Try this quick experiment. Position the ball so that if you drew a straight line back from the ball, it would be positioned off of your left heel. Now move your right foot closer to your left foot so they are about five inches apart. If someone were to look at you, they would swear the ball was in the middle or right of your stance. In reality this is not true, as the ball is still left of center in relation to your body. Your body's position never changed—you just moved your feet closer together. Now assume your regular address, with the ball off the left heel. Instead of moving your right foot closer to your left foot, move your entire body to the left until the ball is in the center of your feet. Do you see the difference? Now your head is directly over the ball, as opposed to being slightly behind it. So for future reference, when I speak of positioning the ball

SPECIAL POINTER FOR WOMEN: *Be sure not to take too wide a stance. When you enlarge the distance between your feet, you are sending a subconscious message to your body to prepare for a big movement. The backswing is for positioning the club, not for winding up the body for power. Women should be particularly careful here since there is already a natural tendency to want to use the body on the backswing. By widening the stance you are encouraging entirely too much body movement.*

between your feet I am talking about changing your body as well as your foot position.

> *Myth:* **At address, tilt your right shoulder so that it is lower than your left.**
>
> *Reality:* **Your grip position dictates the shoulder position.**

Upon the address, the right shoulder is slightly lower than the left. This should be caused by your grip. Do not try to force the shoulder down. It is lower because the right hand grips the club shaft lower than the left hand. The right hand's grip is situated so that the palm of the hand is pointing in the same direction as the club face. If it were pointing downward, that would raise your shoulder, and if it were pointed toward the sky, that would lower your shoulder. Always feel as though both shoulders are level. Nevertheless, realize that from the grip position the right shoulder will actually be lower.

> *Myth:* **Because of their bustlines, all women should have the same position for their arms and hands at the address.**
>
> *Reality:* **Women, like men, have different physical shapes so there is not one standard way for addressing the ball that will work for all women.**

There are two traditional schools of thought on how a woman with a large bust should swing the club on her backswing. One is that she should keep her arms in close to her breasts and swing the club. The other is that she should try to get her arms over her chest to swing the club freely. Neither method is completely correct. Every woman is different in the length of her arms and the size of her bust. There have been very few cases where I have found the bustline to be a real hindrance to the golf swing. In any physique, male or

SPECIAL POINTER FOR WOMEN: If you have a large bustline, I recommend that when bending from your hips, you do not keep your back perfectly straight. Hunch slightly from your shoulders. Your posture will be mildly rounded toward the top of your spine. When you assume this posture, you are placing your breasts closer to your body. If you assume a posture where your back is perfectly straight, your breasts will hang away from your body and could interfere with the arms' swinging freely on your backswing.

female, there are going to be certain proportions that are not ideal for the golf swing. For example, a rotund man with large breasts and short arms is going to be at a greater disadvantage swinging the club than the average female or, for that matter, average male golfer. A skinny male golfer with thin hips cannot swing as well as a female golfer with larger hips and therefore a lower center of gravity.

Alignment

Whenever setting up to your target, aim the club face toward the target. To do this, you must approach the ball from behind. In a straight line, walk toward your ball with the target in mind. Picture a straight line from the ball to the target. Once you feel that the club face is pointing toward your target, align your shoulders, feet, and hips so that they are parallel to the target line. Having the shoulders and hips in parallel alignment every time is very important. The direction in which the shoulders are pointed will affect the plane on which the club is swung back. For example, if your shoulders are pointed to the left, that means the club will be swung on a plane that goes outside the target line (see illustration). If they are pointed toward the right, that means that the club will swing dramatically inside the target line.

When any part of the body is pointed left of the target, we say it is open. If any part of the body is pointed to the right of the target line, we say that it is closed. So you have three positions: open, closed, and parallel. As with the shoulders, any part of the body can assume one of these three positions. For example, your shoulders and feet could be square with the hips in an open position. As was stated earlier, ideally you want the body to be square in its alignment. We have seen how a change in shoulder

Shoulders pointing toward the right at address.

Shoulders pointing toward the left at address.

alignment affects the backswing's path. If the hips' position is open, it means that on the backswing it will be out of sync with the feet and shoulders. If the feet are open or closed, that affects the direction in which the hips will point. So try to keep yourself from looking like a pretzel when you set up to the ball. Just try to keep everything in parallel alignment. Thinking of railroad tracks or laying down your clubs so that one is on your target line seems to help some people. Showing the line of your feet can help too. Anything that you can think of to keep your body in parallel alignment with the ball is worth trying.

A HELPFUL HINT! *When you are forming a mental image of a straight line extending from the ball to the target, pick a spot somewhere along this target line that is close to the ball (see illustration). We call this picking an intermediary target. What you are really doing by picking an intermediary target is moving the target much closer to you, so that if you align the club face with the intermediary target, it will also be aligned with your destination target.*

2

The Grip

Your only link to the club is through your hands. Therefore, the manner in which you grip the club is of the utmost importance. For any golfer—novice to expert—a good grip is the foundation for a good swing.

The grip you will use depends largely on the size of your hands. First, consider what you are gripping, namely the rubber or leather grips on the club. It is my experience that the industry standards for a regular man's and lady's grip are usually too large for the average male or female. If you are a woman of about average hand size and you are having new grips put on your clubs, opt for the slightly undersized grip, for reasons that I will explain later in this chapter.

Now the actual hand position for gripping: *The most important factor in holding the club in the left hand is to make sure the heel of the left hand is on top of the club, not the palm.* The proper grip for the golf club is not written in stone, but the club should be across the fingers and under the

Interlocking grip: The little finger of the right hand interlocks with the index finger of the left hand.

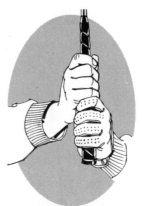

The natural or baseball grip: All four fingers lie on the club.

Overlapping grip: The little finger of the right hand should lie on top and in between the index and second fingers of the left hand.

Let the club lie in the fingers of the right hand. Place the little finger so it lies on top and in between the first and second fingers of the left hand.

Close your hand so the heel of the left hand is on top of the club. The thumb and forefinger should create a *V* that points somewhere between your chin and right shoulder.

The thumb and forefinger of the right hand should form a *V* that points between the chin and right shoulder.

In the left hand place the club so the shaft lies across where the fingers meet the hand. Make sure the left hand is ½" down from the top of the club.

heel of the left hand. This can be done to varying degrees, wherever you are most comfortable. For example, if you were going to throw a stone, you would put the stone not in the palm of your hand but in the fingers. The reason that having the club under the heel of the hand is so important will be addressed in Chapter 5, on generating power. As you will see, creating an angle in the backswing is very important. Having the club under the heel better enables you to cock your wrists on the backswing and, most importantly, to maintain the angle on the down-swing. Experiment for yourself: Place the club more into the palm of your hand and slowly swing the club back to the ball. You will notice that this hand position will promote a casting motion, throwing the club head at the ball rather than maintaining the angle. Now try placing the club under the heel of your hand. You will notice that this makes it easier to maintain the necessary angle. An excellent way to tell if you are holding the club too much in the palm of the hand is by the wear on your glove. If you keep wearing a hole in your glove at the heel of the left hand, this is a sign that you are holding the club too much in the palm of the hand (see illustration). Many women buy brand-new, expensive golf gloves only to have a hole in them by the end of two rounds of golf. Holding the club in the fingers will help your golf game and save you a great deal of expense on golf gloves.

When you first grip the club, have it sitting on the ground so that the bottom of the club face points straight back toward you, making it perpendicular with your feet. Once you get the club face situated, hold on to the tip of the handle with the right hand as you grip it with the left. Once the left hand is holding the club, then grip with your right hand. The reason this is desired is that when you put your left hand on first and then your right hand, there is a tendency to want to twist the club face, pointing it to the

Club placed incorrectly in the palm of the left hand.

Gripping the club while the club is in the air.

left or right. In either case you want that club face's bottom edge to be perpendicular with the line of your feet. Once you get comfortable gripping the club without altering the face's direction, then you might try gripping the club when it is off the ground. Hold your arms away from your body and let the club point into the air at a ninety-degree angle. Now position your hands on the handle. This gives you a better feel for the handle. When the club is sitting on the ground, the weight of the club head can take the feel out of your grip. Also, this method lets you inspect your grip more closely rather than having to lean over to look at your hands. This method of club gripping will definitely increase your sensitivity to pressure points and will give you a better visual perspective of where your hands are on the club.

> *Myth:* **Women must lock the club in the palms of their hands because they lack arm and hand strength.**
>
> *Reality:* **Putting the club in the palm of your hands has a devastating effect in the full swing. To swing correctly you should have the heel of the left hand on top of the club and the fingers of the right hand gripping the club.**

One of the most common errors with beginners and many women of various levels is the tendency to apply a death grip to the club. By a death grip I mean squeezing with the whole hand instead of using different pressure points. If you grip the club in the palm of your hand, you will find it almost impossible not to squeeze with the whole hand. However, if you place the club in the fingers, you can apply pressure to certain areas and still hold on to the club. Many women put the club in the palm of their hand because of their lack of upper body strength. This grip gives them the sensation that they are holding on to the club firmly and are in control of swinging the club. With a palm grip, they are indeed holding on to the club firmly, but unfortunately, this firmness is actually giving them less control over the club. When the hands tense up too much, the forearms become stiff and the golfer loses the ability to swing the club.

Always remember that golf is a *swinging* motion, not a *contrived* motion. Its control comes from an apparent lack of control. A tight grip forces the body to use the larger muscles on the backswing. When you use the larger muscles of the body, it is the same as using the whole body. You must remember that on the backswing all you want to do is to swing the club back into a position. The more you throw your body into the backswing, the less likelihood there is that the club will be in the same position every time. Remember, *for women there is already a natural tendency to use the whole body, so it is important not to exaggerate this movement.* Also, with rigid hands, the wrists cannot cock as they should. On the backswing you should do two things: Turn your shoulders and cock your wrists. With stiff hands and forearms you cannot accomplish the latter.

Let me explain the location of the pressure points that I have been describing. First, in the left hand you should feel pressure in the last three fingers of the hand. When the heel of the hand is on top of the club and the last three fingers are applying most of the pressure, you will be creating a viselike effect. This is particularly important in maintaining the angle on the downswing. The thumb of the left hand should be off to the right side, with a slight touch of pressure between the thumb and the forefinger of the left hand. With the right hand, once the club has been placed in the middle

Swing the club while holding it with just three fingers in the right hand.

Holding the club with the heel and index finger of the left hand.

joint of the fingers, they should curl around the grip, with the middle two fingers providing most of the pressure. The thumb should be off to the left side with a touch of pressure between the thumb and forefinger of the right hand. Also, the thumb of the left hand should fit snugly into the palm of the right hand. *During address or during the swing you should not feel a large amount of pressure on the thumb of the left hand from the palm of the right.*

The difficult part in describing the grip is that tightness and pressure are relative terms. The most important thing is to know what you want the grip to accomplish in the swing. If you have a good idea of what you want to accomplish, you can figure out for yourself what amount of pressure is correct.

Exercises: There are a couple of good exercises to practice the correct grip tension and pressure points. Both exercises are one-handed drills designed to teach each hand its proper role in the swing. For the right hand, hold the club in the second joint of the middle three fingers and swing the club without the thumb or the little finger on the club. The purpose of this exercise is to make you realize that you can hold on to the club with just a few fingers. Once you understand this, when you grip with the whole hand, you will tend to relax the hand and use the fingers as the grip.

With the left hand, place the club so the heel of the hand is on top and try to swing the club, with the index finger acting as a support. Again, once you realize you can swing the club with just one hand, there will be less of a tendency to grip so tightly with the whole hand.

Changing Your Grip

One of the hardest parts of the golf swing to change is your grip, particularly if you have been gripping the club incorrectly for many years. The only contact you have with the club is through your hands, and once they are secure in their positioning, they will not change easily. I have watched golfers who, when attempting to change their grips, seconds before their take-away their hands will unconsciously slide back into their old position. Realize that when you do change your grip, your hands will have to relearn how to swing through correctly. For a period of time you might hit some dramatic shots (like a slice or a hook), so it is best to work with your grip change at a driving range. Hit a large bucket of balls with no other swing thought than how to correctly grip the club. Do not worry about where the ball is going; just concentrate on your grip. As I stated, it will be a while before your hands relearn how to react when swinging through your shot.

If you do not have time to go to a driving range, here is a good practice that can be done in your home. While you are watching television or whenever you get a free moment, pick up the club and grip it. You do not have to swing it; just grip it and look at your hands' position. Play around with different pressure points, trying to apply pressure with your fingers. Do this maybe fifteen minutes a day, and in a couple of weeks you'll be swinging with a new grip. The true test will be when you set foot on the golf course. Your first reaction will be to immediately revert to your old grip. Try to fight this inclination as best you can. Expect to have a few bad rounds; do not get upset. Sacrificing a few bad rounds of golf is well worth a drop in your score!

SPECIAL POINTER FOR WOMEN: *For all of you women who have heard innumerable times, "You bent your left arm! If you had only kept it straight, the ball would have gone 10 yards farther!" you will find in later chapters that this is not true. You do not need a perfectly straight left arm. Nevertheless, if you grip the club correctly, your left arm will naturally straighten out. Grip the club in the left hand. Lay the club so that the fingers are pointing toward the ground and the club is lying across where the fingers meet the hand. Now take the heel of the hand and place it on top of the club. You will immediately feel the left arm straighten. Yet the great thing about it is that the arm is straight— not from tension, but because the manner in which you contorted your arm forces it to be so. Try this little trick and you will not have to listen to "Don't bend your left arm; keep it straight."*

• • •

3

The Backswing

*There are two major parts to the golf
swing: the backswing and the
downswing. As its name implies, the
backswing consists of literally swinging
the club back. When the backswing is
executed correctly, your club and body
will be set in a position that will enable
you to initiate a proper downswing.*

When you are executing the backswing, there are two
things you want to accomplish: a full shoulder turn
(ninety degrees) and the cocking of the wrists. Any other
movement that occurs should be the result of the turning
of the shoulders or the cocking of the wrists. For example,
in a relaxed state, standing completely erect, turn your
shoulders to the right. You will notice when you do so
that your hips start turning after the shoulders have
rotated about forty-five degrees. This is perfectly natural.
Obviously, your upper and lower body are attached, and
when the upper body turns, this will force the lower
body to turn with it. You should not try to turn your hips,
and on the other hand, you do not want to restrict the

hips' movement. The lower body should respond to the upper body's movement. You might want to think of the lower body as being a base on which the upper body turns. When you turn your shoulders, both feet should remain on the ground. This means the left heel does not lift into the air.

Let me explain why keeping your left heel on the ground during the backswing will be important. Again, stand erect and turn your shoulders to the right about ninety degrees. Your hips will turn about forty-five degrees. Now lift your left heel about one inch off the ground. Do you feel your lower body losing any tension or resistance to the upper body's turning? We do not want this! Ideally, there should be torque, or tension, between the upper and lower body.

> *Myth:* **To get more distance, really turn those shoulders!**
>
> *Reality:* **For most people the maximum amount of shoulder turn should be ninety degrees. Anything more throws the body out of position and results in a loss of power.**

The turning of the shoulders should be a light, brisk move. Often instructors tell students to twist until it is uncomfortable. *Wrong!* For golfers with a normal amount of flexion in their upper body, the shoulder turn is a rhythmic turn, with the concentration being on the shoulder caps' rotating ninety degrees. Remember as a child singing, "I'm a little tea cup, short and stout?" Put both your hands on your shoulders (forget the spout), as you did when you sang this song. Now rotate your shoulder caps ninety degrees. This is all that is necessary for completing the shoulder turn. No special contortions are required. When you turn your shoulders, be careful that you are turning them on a level plane. If you look at

Stand level with the club
behind your shoulders.

Turn shoulders 90 degrees.

Bend from hips with the club
behind your shoulders.

Turn shoulders.

Notice how the wrists cock vertically.

professional golfers, it will appear that their shoulders are turning under on the backswing, but in reality they are turning level. Stand erect and place the shaft of the club behind your shoulders, parallel to the ground. Now turn. Your shoulders are turning level, correct? Next, tilt thirty-five degrees from your hips and turn your shoulders. Your shoulders are still turning level—it is just that your body's angle is tilted. So whenever you turn your shoulders, do not intentionally turn them under.

To summarize, you must do two things on the backswing: Turn your shoulders and cock your wrists. Anything else that happens in the backswing occurs because one of these two motions has made it happen.

Now, to the wrist cock. *As the shoulders are turning, the wrists should be cocking vertically* (first illustration). Stand erect and put your arms straight out from your body. Hold a golf club so that the arms and the club are in a straight line and are parallel with the ground. Then cock your wrists so that the club is perpendicular to the ground, pointing straight toward the sky. This is the correct wrist cock. Then make your shoulder turn, and position the club so that it is parallel with the ground. This is the correct position to be in at the top of the backswing. Now put yourself in your address and start your backswing with the shoulders turning. As soon as you start turning the shoulders, you can begin to cock your wrists. If you will remember in Chapter 1 on the address, I spoke of the hands' being in a precocked position at setup. This is exactly why you want them precocked. With them slightly cocked at address, all you will have to do is hinge them in about a half-inch more and they will be fully cocked.

Experiment for yourself. Address the ball with your arms and wrists in a straight line, and start turning your shoulders. From this point you will have to cock your wrists the full ninety degrees. Now start in the position that I have suggested (where the wrists form about a forty-five degree angle with the shaft of the club). You

The address with the wrists in a precocked position.

will notice that when you turn your shoulders about forty-five degrees the club is pointing toward the sky without your having to move your wrists at all. If you let the hands continue on their course to about ear level, the club will be almost parallel to the ground. You will also see where the importance of your grip will come into play. When you have the heel of the left hand on top of the club's shaft, all you need to do is apply a little downward pressure with this heel and your hands will be fully cocked.

The fact that we hold the club in the fingers of our hands also facilitates this movement. Since the thumbs are positioned off to the sides of the shaft, there should be no thumb pressure to keep the wrists from cocking. Again, experiment for yourself. When gripping the club, place both thumbs directly down the top of the shaft in a straight line and apply pressure with the thumbs on the shaft. Now swing the club back and try to cock your wrists. When you do so you should feel the thumbs offering resistance, and this is precisely what we do not want. The way the wrists cock will also affect the positioning of the club head. At the top of the backswing we want the club head to be in an open position. This means the bottom line of the club face will be perpendicular to the ground (see illustration). If your wrists cock vertically, this will happen.

However, notice what happens when your wrists cock so that the back of the left hand at the wrist area is completely flat. This closes the club face. A club face is closed when the face points toward the sky. This is an undesirable position. When the club face points completely toward the sky, we call this completely closed, or dead shut. However, there can be varying degrees of being closed. One such example is the square club face (see illustration). It is halfway between

Arms in a straight line with the shaft of the club.

Club face in an open position.

Club face in a square position.

the open and closed faces and can be an effective position for some swings. On the other side of the spectrum, we have a super-open club face. This occurs when in the process of the wrist cock the wrist of the right hand remains flat rather than assuming its desired concave position (see illustration). If you experiment with each of these positions by swinging down toward the ball you will note that each position has the club face pointing in a different direction at impact. The position we want the club to be in at impact is the same in which we addressed the ball, which is the club face pointing directly toward the target. So you see, the club head position created by the cocking of the wrists is going to be very important!

The direction in which the shaft of the club points at the top of the backswing is also important. Ideally, at the top of your swing the shaft of the club should be pointing down the target line. This will occur if the hands follow the shoulders' path and the wrists cock correctly, and of course, if your body is aligned correctly to begin with (see Chapter 1 on alignment). However, there are two different directions the club could point to at the top of the swing. If the club points to the right of your target at the top of your backswing, we say that the club is across the line. (see illustration on page 21.) This position is usually reached by swinging the club too far on an inside path, so that when it reaches the top it points to the right. There is an old saying that the ball will go in the direction in which the club head points; this is not always true, but in this instance it could well be the case.

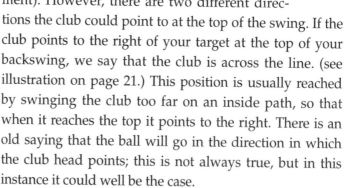

Closed club face.

Shaft of club parallel to target line.

With the club head pointing far off to the right, chances are that when you swing back through, the ball will also go straight to the right. This is a pushed shot, which occurs when your club's shaft points in the wrong direction at the swing's top. When the club points off to the left we say the club is laid off. This will happen when, on the backswing, the club takes a path that is outside its normal path, thus leading it to point to the left. If the club returns on this path on the downswing, it will move from the outside to the inside, creating a slice or a pull. A pulled shot is one that goes dead left of your target. It is caused by the club swinging from the right to the left across the target line, which creates a pulling sensation, hence the name pull. A slice occurs when the ball starts out toward your target but then veers sharply to the right. It is caused by the same mechanical error that creates a pulled shot. The difference between the two is, with the slice, at impact the club face is pointing toward the target. With a pull, at impact the club face is pointing left of the target.

It is not always wrong or bad to have the club point off to the right or left if the person swinging the club manages to get it on plane on the downswing. It also depends on how severely the shaft is offline. If the club points slightly to the right or left, it might be just fine. However, when your club is pointing twenty-five degrees or more, you are probably going to be in trouble. So now, in addition to noting how your club head is positioned, you should also pay attention to where the shaft of the club is pointing.

On the backswing the left arm should dominate. The club should literally be swung back, with the left arm leading and the right arm going along for the ride. The left wrist should initiate the wrist cock. As I suggested earlier, you might feel the pressure that starts the cocking of the left wrist coming from the heel of the left hand. Many right-handed golfers are very right-hand dominant. By right-hand dominant I mean that the strength between the two arms is dramatically disproportionate, with the right arm dominating. One way to tell if you are too right-hand dominant is to look at the position of your right elbow at

Shaft of club "across the line."

Shaft of club "laid off."

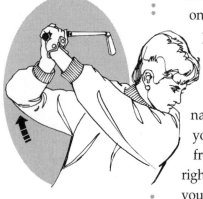

Flying right elbow.

the top of your backswing. If the right elbow sticks out toward the side or the sky, your right arm is dominating on the backswing. Another indicator is that at the top of your backswing your hands should be extended from your body as they were at address. If you feel that your left elbow is collapsing at the top of your swing, this may be because the right hand is dominating the wrist cock and pulling the club in toward your body. Another form of right-arm dominance comes from being completely visually coordinated with your right side and having very little visual coordination with your left side. Either way such dominance is not good for the golf swing unless you can train the right hand and arm to perform their proper role in the golf swing.

One way to cure the first example of right-hand dominance is to strengthen your left hand and arm. An exercise such as squeezing a tennis ball or lifting light weights will help. Whenever you are on the golf course and waiting to hit your next shot, hold the club with your left hand and make several full swings. You will be able to tell from this little exercise how much strength you actually have in your left arm. If you can get to the top of your backswing and follow through without difficulty, strength is not your problem. However, very few right-handed golfers are able to do this without practice. Whenever possible, practice the left-handed swing. It will build muscles in your left arm rather quickly.

Lack of visual coordination is not as serious as lack of strength. On your backswing the left arm really does not require a lot of coordination. Its whole purpose is simply to remain extended from your body and allow the left wrist to cock. However, if your left side is disproportionately uncoordinated, this will make it difficult for your left arm to take dominance over the right on the backswing.

One way I suggest to increase your coordination in your left arm is simply to use it. When you are at work or at home, try to do any simple task with your left hand.

For example, when you reach for a spoon or a glass, lift with your left hand and then place the object in your right hand. If you consciously stick with this for a couple of weeks, you will be surprised at how much quicker your left side will begin to interact with your right. And just through doing these simple tasks, your arm and hand will start to develop more strength. You might even find that your left hand works better at certain tasks, and after doing this for a period of time you might start to reach for items unconsciously with your left hand!

Keep in mind that you are doing all these exercises to balance out the difference in dominance between the two arms. Do not get confused. We want the right arm to be strong in the swing; we are not trying to weaken it, but rather to strengthen the left arm to create a balance. Another way to lessen the difference between your arms is to train your right arm to become submissive. The best way to accomplish this is through one-handed drills. Take the club in your right hand and swing it back into your desired position. Do this any time you are on the golf course and in between shots, and when you are at the driving range. You can also hit balls with this one-hand exercise. But remember, if the trouble is with your backswing, that is where you should concentrate; do not worry about making contact with the ball.

Be Careful: Although it is fine to let the heel of the left hand initiate the wrist cock, make sure that it does not pull your left shoulder down. It is not unusual to see someone who is applying too much downward pressure with the heel of the left hand to drop her left shoulder on the backswing. Also always make sure the shoulders have started turning before you attempt to cock your wrists. When you cock the wrists first, this puts the club on the wrong arc and is commonly referred to as picking the club up. Remember: shoulders, then wrists.

As the left arm leads on the backswing and the wrists begin to cock, the right arm is also going to bend. The right arm should bend so that the forearm and bicep resemble the letter *L*. Your right elbow should point toward the ground. Since you are right-handed, there will be the tendency for the right hand to try to dominate on the backswing. This usually results in the right elbow pointing toward the sky. Just remember to relax the right arm and let it go along for the ride, and it should bend correctly.

As all this is happening you will feel your weight getting pulled over to the right side. This is perfectly normal. Remember that your lower body is just a base on which the upper body is turning, and its job is simply to respond. So make sure that as you swing back your knees remain flexed. This is particularly true for the right knee. Many golfers have a strong tendency to straighten the knee on the backswing. If you try to keep your knee flexed but it continues to straighten, this is probably being caused by some other incorrect move that you are making (see Chapter 11 on troubleshooting). You should feel your left knee move slightly toward your right knee as your shoulders turn. The knees should always remain fairly level with one another and if you feel the left knee going downward you will know that this is incorrect.

I mentioned the fact that when the shoulders turn, this forces the hips to also turn. If you stand straight and turn your shoulders, you will feel the left hipbone turning in toward the right hipbone. Now when you bend over and make the same turn, this should happen again. The reason I am mentioning this is that sometimes when you bend you segment your body so that it does not work together as one unit, which is what you want, because the shoulders should turn farther than the hips. But sometimes, unless you make sure your left hipbone moves toward your right hipbone, your upper body will push away from your lower body, leaving the hip sticking out. Not only is this funny-looking, but it is also quite uncomfortable! If you have a mirror handy, rehearse turning your shoulders while standing straight and then in your address position. The hips should move the same in either position.

On the backswing, the hands should swing to about ear level by the time the shoulders have made their full ninety-degree turn.

> *Myth:* **The backswing should be a one-piece movement.**
>
> *Reality:* **The shoulders and arms should be moving at two different speeds.**

Many golfers try to employ what is called a one-piece take-away the idea being that the shoulders, arms, and hands all move together, with the shoulders directing the show. To some degree this is true. However, I cannot ever remember anyone who has used this swing thought, and actually swung the club back correctly. They all had the same faults with their back-swings, which I will now describe. When golfers visualize a one-piece take-away, they imagine the arms and hands all moving together with the shoulders. The mistake that they make is that they swing this whole group back at the same speed. This leads to an over-swing, and usually a reverse pivot. The arms, hands, and shoulders do not swing at the same speed. The arms must swing faster than the shoulders.

Stand erect and place a club across your collarbone so that it is parallel with the ground. Now turn your shoulders ninety degrees. You will notice that your shoulders make this turn fairly quickly. Now assume your regular address position, and swing the hands until they are at ear level. Your arms and hands have much farther to travel than the shoulders, so consequently the arms and hands must move faster than the shoulders on the backswing. When you try to take them back at the same speed, here is what happens. When you address the ball, your thought is at the top of your backswing to have the club parallel with the ground. OK, now you swing the club back, arms and shoulders at the same speed. Now your shoulders have turned ninety degrees, only your hands are not near ear level and the shaft of the club is not parallel with the ground. What you will end up having to do is keep turning your shoulders until the arms and hands are in position. When you do this, you will end up with your shoulders turned well past ninety degrees, which is an overswing. The shoulders have turned too much and have now thrown your weight onto your left side, which creates a reverse pivot (see illustration).

When I see one of my students displaying this type of positioning, my first question is, "Are you trying to swing the club with a one-piece take-away?" Nine times out of ten she will look at me and ask, "How did you know? I read in a golf magazine that it was important to take the club back in one piece." There are, of course, different variations on this story. Some will say they read it somewhere, or perhaps a golf professional or their husband had told them to. Either way, this "swing thought" leads to trouble. (A swing thought is a mental image of what you want to accomplish.)

Take the club and hold it with your right hand and just let it swing freely back and forth. This is the speed your arms should be swinging. It is important that your shoulders turn and set the path on which the arms are going to move. Yet, as I have shown you, the shoulder turn is a light, brisk move and there is just no way the hands can cover all the area they must cover if they move at the same speed as the shoulders. You might want to read Chapter 3 on the forward press. This will help get the arms swinging at a faster rate. You might also want to read Chapter 12 on exercises and try the one-handed drills, as well as the press-forward drill, the swinging-arms drill, and if you can find someone to assist you, the two-person drill. The two-person drill is

Reverse pivot.

an excellent drill to get you to feel how fast your arms should be swinging.

> *Myth:* **Take the club straight back for the first 12 inches.**
>
> *Reality:* **You never take the club straight back; the shoulder turn will dictate the club's path.**

A frequently asked question is "How do I get the club set on the correct swing plane going back?" The answer is, you don't. If you simply turn your shoulders and allow your wrists to cock vertically, this will put you on the correct swing plane. The hands should always maintain the same position relative to the body that they had at address. You should not feel your hands increasing in distance from your body and you do not want them to come closer. Never try to take the club straight back with the hands and arms. The shoulder turn will put the club on the correct swing path. All that is required of the hands is to allow the wrists to cock. The hands will simply follow the wrists' vertical movement, going up, not around, the body.

Another very important consideration is the posture you created at the address. *When the wrists are cocking vertically, do not pull your body up out of your posture. Remain on the same tilted axis as in your address.* The backswing is the shoulders' turning and wrists' cocking, not the lifting of your body out of its posture. The backswing is for power, but we obtain that power through proper club position at the top of the swing. If the club is in the proper position and all the body parts have turned in the correct manner, you are halfway to having the ideal golf shot. It is really amazing how little effort should go into the backswing. It is physics more than muscle power that obtains distance. Think of when you hit your best golf shot and it felt as though you had done nothing. That is the way it should always feel. The only way that you should find golf tiring is from the emotional drain of concentration, or the physical side of walking, or other nonswing-related exertion (like spending the day looking for your golf ball). If you come in after a leisurely round of golf and feel exhausted, there is something definitely wrong with your swing. *It should never require that much exertion!*

The Overrated Weight Shift

Myth: **Consciously shift your weight to the right foot on your backswing.**

Reality: **If you are executing the backswing correctly, your weight should shift naturally.**

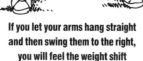

If you let your arms hang straight and then swing them to the right, you will feel the weight shift naturally to the right.

Arms have swung to the right.

If you are a beginning to intermediate golfer, I am sure someone has told you at one time to shift your weight to your right side on your backswing. This is a very commonly taught idea and a very incorrect one. It is true that your weight does shift to the right on the backswing. Nevertheless, it is not a forced weight shift. When your shoulders turn and your hands swing to the right, this slight motion is enough to give you all the weight shift you need. There are two things you should not do: restrict the weight shift, which will lead to a reverse pivot; and force the weight to shift, which will lead to a sway.

Whenever someone comes to me with the problem of swaying off the ball (head and body sway to the right on the backswing), I ask if they have been working on getting their weight over to the right side on their backswing. Almost always they say yes, because a golf professional had told them to force the weight to shift. As I stated earlier, the weight will move to the right when the hands swing with the wrists' cocking vertically. However, in order for the weight to move correctly the right leg must remain flexed. With the right knee in a flexed position, it can receive the weight as the hands swing and the wrists cock. If the right leg is locked straight there is no way the right leg can receive the weight shift without making the body sway on the backswing. Experiment yourself: Without a club, assume your address position with your arms hanging. Then put the palms of your hands together in a praying position. Turn your shoulders and let your arms swing to the right. As soon as you do this, you should also feel your weight shift toward the right. The simple act of turning and letting your arms swing provides enough momentum to shift your weight.

The Unnatural "Nature" of the Swing

Both men and women find a certain unnaturalness to the golf swing. Although I believe women rank much higher than men in their natural ability for golf, there are pitfalls for both sexes. In the golf swing there is a tendency to want to generate power with the strongest part of the anatomy. The body will want to use ways to create power that are incorrect even in the strongest of athletes.

One way this occurs is when the body tries to use leverage to create power. An example of this would be the tendency to raise the body on the backswing, actually lifting oneself out of one's original posture, trying to create power. I think at some point almost every golfer has been told, "You're lifting up," referring either to their backswing or their downswing. Instead of getting upset when this happens to you, realize that it is your body's

SPECIAL POINTER FOR WOMEN: *The problem of women swaying off the ball is very common and usually happens for the reason just mentioned: Someone has told them to make sure they shift their weight over to the right foot, and the result is a sway. Do not worry about the weight shift. If you execute the backswing correctly, the weight will shift naturally.*

natural way of trying to help. In any other sport it probably would be beneficial, but unfortunately in golf this natural instinct is harmful.

Another natural tendency is to want to throw the club head at the ball. To create power, it is necessary to maintain the angle at the top of your backswing. However, every instinct in your body is going to want to do otherwise. Most people want to throw the club head at the ball instead of delaying the release of the hands. This early release of the hands almost certainly will be accompanied by the lifting of the body. In fact, they go hand in hand and create a swing that you frequently see on the practice tee. Often the person who is with the one practicing will be very judgmental and say something like, "Martha, you didn't keep your head down," and, "Stop chopping at the ball!" Well, Martha, it wasn't your fault. It's just your body's instinctive way to try to create energy.

Another very unnatural movement occurs in the backswing. In many athletic motions it is normal for the hands to want to swing on the same plane as the shoulders. When the shoulders turn on a horizontal plane, the hands want to swing with them on the same plane. If the shoulders turn on a steep vertical plane, again the hands like to follow (see illustration). However, in golf this motion is incorrect. In the backswing, as the shoulders are turning the wrists and hands should be moving vertically in relation to the tilt of the shoulders (see illustration). This is often a confusing movement to people who have a strong orientation toward the shoulders and hands traveling on the same plane.

This is why many people say the golf swing is so unnatural: It is unnatural because the normal ways you would generate power do not work in the golf swing. So far the examples I have given have shown the gender differences. Men, having upper body strength, tend to slash at the ball, and women, lacking this strength, tend to use tempo and timing to create the

Arms swinging with the shoulders as they turn horizontally.

Arms swinging with the shoulders on a steep plane.

golf swing. There are also individual differences. If you are a woman with very strong, quick legs, there will be a tendency for them to try to dominate during your swing. If you have exceptionally strong hands (in relation to the other parts of your body), your hands may try to dominate.

One way this could occur is by picking the club up on the backswing instead of allowing the shoulders to initiate the swing (see Chapter 11 on troubleshooting). And the woman with strong, quick legs could well have a problem with her lower body's getting too far ahead on the downswing.

One woman who comes to me for golf lessons has exceptionally strong hands and a very petite build. She also has a chronic problem of snatching the club on the backswing. I had a male friend whose hands were fast and coordinated, but in comparison his legs were very slow to respond. I brought this to his attention one day by saying, "Your hand-eye coordination is incredible, but your legs just don't seem to want to move." He replied, "That's been the case since I was in high school. I'm great in ping-pong and would have been great in tennis, but my legs never responded quickly enough." One way to compensate for the stronger part of the body that wants to dominate is to try to increase the strength in the weaker part. For example, I suggested to the woman who had the very strong hands to increase her strength in her biceps and shoulders. However, she felt that she did not possess enough innate strength in her upper body to really help. I then suggested that she increase her leg strength, the idea being to increase strength in any of the weaker parts of the body to keep one area like the hands from dominating. For myself, I have very strong, quick legs and occasionally they try to get involved too much with my swing. But over the years I have had to work very hard to teach them to respond to the upper body, not to dictate my swing.

Wrists hinge as the shoulders turn.

SPECIAL POINTER FOR WOMEN: *If you are a woman with a large bustline and are swinging the club back with the arms and hands traveling on the same plane, the arms and hands must move in a vertical manner as shown or you will never be able to get back to the ball.*

Everyone from Jack Nicklaus on down has some idiosyncrasy with their swing that stems from their personal physical attributes. As I stated earlier, in the general swing motion women are definitely at an advantage. However, as you get more individualized, your own physical strengths and weaknesses, will affect your swing.

Tempo and Timing

Myth: **To create power, it is necessary for a woman to take the club back slowly.**

Reality: **There is a definite distinction between taking the club back and swinging the club away. If you take the club back slowly, it becomes a contrived motion. What we want in golf is a swinging motion. Its sense of control is its lack of control.**

First, let me define a tempo. The tempo is the speed at which you swing a golf club. You never want to guide the club on the backswing or the downswing. You must swing the club at a tempo that is on a continuum somewhere between slow and fast. You know you have swung a club too slowly if you are "thinking the club back," trying physically to guide its swing path.

The only way you can swing a club too quickly is if it affects your timing. (The definition of timing is the relationship of the hands swinging to the movement of the body.) If you swing the club back so quickly that at the top of your backswing you are out of balance because of the momentum created by the speed of the swinging club, it is very difficult for your hands and body to get back in sync to hit the ball.

As you will see, balance is a harmony created by tempo and timing. If you are not in balance with the proper ratio of weight on the left and right feet, you will have trouble executing a downswing.

A tempo pattern that seems to help many golfers is to actually think of a rhythm on their backswing. The tempo "one-two-and-three" defines the swing motion fairly well. For example, make your forward press a "one" count. Your backswing is the "two" count. The "and" is a slight hesitation that occurs at the top of your backswing. The "three" will be your downswing. You might want to repeat this count to yourself, whenever you are hitting balls. Make sure that you don't forget the "and." It represents a change of direction that occurs at the top of your swing. If you'd like, lengthen the two, making it "one, two, and three." This allows you a little more time to swing the club back. Whatever amount of time you want to assign to any part, just try to keep all four parts rhythmic, and symmetrical.

If you are having problems establishing a tempo, it could be from some swing faults. I often hear golfers say, "If I could only slow down my swing, I would hit the ball better." If you feel yourself rushing through your swing, it is probably because of a swing fault. If you feel that you are rushing your backswing, it could be that you are swinging the club back with too much momentum. Momentum and speed can be two different things. Speed is the rate at which you are swinging. Momentum is when you put mass behind this speed. So when you feel your backswing moving quickly, it could be a result of putting too much of your body into the swing. Remember, you want your shoulders, arms, and wrists to swing the could, not your whole body.

Another factor that can make your backswing feel rushed is from not completing your shoulder turn. If your shoulders do not turn ninety degrees, this will give you the sensation that you are swinging very quickly. In reality, you have shortend your backswing, which, of course, will make it feel faster. Another possibility is that you are not turning your shoulders at all. When your shoulders do not turn, you will lift the club with your arms and wrists. Again, this will create a fast backswing because you have left out an essential part of the swing, the shoulder turn.

On your downswing if you feel the club lashing through at the ball, it is definitely a problem with your swing. When you do not complete the shoulder turn on your backswing, this shortens your swing so you will feel yourself rushing through the shot. An incomplete shoulder turn gives you the sensation of hacking or chopping at the ball on your follow-through. One of the most common problems that create a quick downswing is throwing the club head at the ball. If you remember, what creates power in the golf swing is the delay of the release of the angle. This means you never want to try to force the club head to do anything. You want to swing the handle of the club at the ball (not the club head itself, which will give you a slashing sensation). Men are usually the ones to complain about a fast downswing. It is natural for men to try to use forearm and hand strength to make the ball go far. However, when attempting to use their forearm strength they end up slashing at the ball, by throwing the club head. Women, on the other hand, do not tend to slash at the ball because of their natural inclination to use timing and body movement to create power.

The Effortless Swing

When you hit your best shot, you will notice that it feels effortless. Your conscious effort at creating timing did not produce this shot. It was good mechanics that created the excellent timing. Even though I have asked

SPECIAL POINTER FOR WOMEN: Since many women lack forearm and hand strength, there is a tendency to try to generate power in the backswing by forcing the whole body into the backswing. This will not increase power! The idea of the backswing is to get the club into a position that will enable you to create power on the downswing.

you to set yourself into a rhythm such as "one, two, and three," this in itself will not produce a good shot. But it is possible that if you repeat this to yourself enough times, your mechanics will try to adjust to your timing, and as your mechanics improve so will your timing. So you see, they will work hand in hand as your swing improves. When you hit a ball farther than you have ever hit it before, it is wonderful to watch. What is even better is the feeling that you have not expended any energy. This goes back to the theory that the golf swing is not produced by muscle but by letting your club do the work for you. Whenever I teach beginners, they are always amazed when they hit their first effortless shot. "That felt like nothing" is a commonplace comment. "This," I tell them, "is the first time that you are really understanding what the golf swing is about." This fluidity is produced in any sport when you get the most amount of energy out of the least amount of effort. There is no superfluous motion; it all works as one. I think that golf, of all sports, provides one of the more effortless motions because of the physics involved with the swing. There are very few sports where an instrument such as a golf club becomes the core of your motion, with your body doing everything it can to enhance the club's ability to swing. The golf swing should feel as easy as it looks; unfortunately, it takes a lot of work before one acquires that ease.

Balance and Symmetry

Myth: The anatomical design of a woman is not conducive to the golf swing.

Reality: Women actually have an advantage staying in balance on the golf swing due to a lower center of gravity created by the hips.

Having a sense of balance and symmetry on the backswing is very important. This symmetry and balance have in one part been created by timing and tempo. The hips provide a lower center of gravity that comes in handy when it comes to golf. This lower center combined with a woman's natural tendency to use the whole body work well together. You might think of the hips as having an anchoring effect, allowing a woman to use more body motion and timing to generate power. Unfortunately, women are taught to use their hips as a source of power. Women are told to really wind up those hips on the backswing and let them spin on the downswing. This will give you the sensation that you're going to create power, but that sensation is misleading. The twisting and coiling of your hips is throwing them out of position and is not helping your backswing. *The most important function of the backswing is to put the club in a stable position. You should swing the club back for position, not for power.* In other words, you should not feel yourself twisting, winding, or exerting a great deal of energy with your body. Ideally you want to be in balance and control at the top of your swing, and the hips provide that balance.

Golf as a Reactive Motion

One of the things that makes the golf swing such a difficult motion to repeat is that it is not a reaction to a stimulus. Rather the motion has to be initiated. If someone throws something at you, you react without going through a conscious process. You either duck, try to catch it, or possibly stop it. I have always felt that golf would be a lot easier to learn if someone would roll the ball toward you and you simply reacted by swinging at it.

Unfortunately, in golf we start from a stationary position and have to initiate our own motion through a conscious effort. Ideally, the ultimate goal is to make golf a reaction rather than a consciously performed action. A beginner must think about every move that is made, while the seasoned professional will concentrate on external variables such as positioning and target orientation, relying more on a conditioned response, or you might say on muscle memory. In a given situation, a professional's body has learned how to react instinctively to the situation.

There are several ways a golfer can try to make golf a reaction, rather than a contrived motion. One of these is to establish a forward press. A forward press is a movement that initiates the backswing by slightly pressing part of the body forward. This simple press of the body toward the target helps initiate an automatic reaction. You might even think of it as pushing in one direction to rebound in another; for example, pressing the hands slightly forward makes it easier for them to swing back. There are many different types of forward presses, and they vary as much as the individuals who use them. The most famous forward press might be Sam Snead's swiveling of the head slightly to the right and then pressing the right knee toward the target just before the take-away. (The take-away is golf lingo for the start of the backswing. It is named as such because the club is swung, or taken away from the ball.) Whatever your forward press might be, realize that it is an action used to create a reaction.

Individualizing Your Forward Press

If you are completely still before you start your backswing and want to establish a forward press, here's how to do it. First, to establish what part of your body you are going to press forward, you have to evaluate the strengths and weaknesses of your swing. For example, if you tend to use too much lower body movement on the backswing, you might want to forward press with your hands. By doing so you are triggering the upper body to start the backswing, not the lower body. If your hands tend to be much faster than the rest of your body, on the backswing you might want to try pressing forward with the lower body. Whichever part of the body that you press forward will usually be the first to initiate the backswing. By pressing forward I am referring to a slight, subtle motion—just enough to trigger the backswing. The more you press forward, the more you will tend to exaggerate the opposite motion of the press. For example, if you make a large press with your legs forward, there will be a tendency to use too much of your legs on your backswing. So you see, it is important to use this press as a subtle trigger.

To help put you in some sort of rhythm you might want to think of the press as a "one" count, the backswing as "two," the change of directions as "and," and the downswing as "three." So your swing would have the tempo "one, two, and three," the "and" being a slight hesitation at the top of your backswing.

If you are using the hands as a forward press, make sure you do not alter the position of the club face from your setup. Some people start out with their hands slightly behind the ball and then press forward into position. If you start with your hands in the correct position and then press forward chances are you will push the club face into an open position. With the club head in the correct position at the address you want to make a slight press of the left hand toward your target and be careful not to alter the club face's position. Usually, when left alone, new golfers will establish their own presses without even being aware that they are doing so. However, if you are a rigid mechanical player, chances are you don't have a press, so you will have to consciously make an effort to create one.

SPECIAL POINTER FOR WOMEN: *Most women lack a certain degree of upper body strength. Since there is already a natural tendency to use the whole body on the backswing, you must be very careful what part of your body you are going to press forward. Do not try to use a full body press. (A full body press is when the entire left side of the body is pressed toward the target.) This press will usually result in entirely too much body movement in the backswing.*

Pumping the Arms

An important preface to the forward press is the pumping of the forearms and the tapping of the feet (see illustration). If you recall, at the address, we want the arms hanging straight, but this straightness is caused by gravity, not by tension. A good way to take tension out of the arms is to pump them from the elbows. By pumping I mean once you are set up, move your hands up toward your stomach about 4 inches and then let them hang straight. Do this four or five times before your take-away. In conjunction with the arms' pumping you want the feet to tap. To tap your feet, first lift your left heel about three-quarters of an inch off the ground and replace it. Then lift your right heel the same amount and replace it. You will want to do this four or five times. As you are doing this, you will feel your weight shift from your left foot to your right foot, back and forth. The tapping of the feet is simply to wake up your lower body and prepare it for making an athletic motion. For example, in baseball, basketball, tennis, and any number of sports, you do not stand flat-footed. You will naturally rock back and forth from the right to left foot. This is a unconscious action to prepare you for movement in any direction. Since the golf swing begins as a conscious effort, you must train your feet and arms to be prepared for the athletic motion that is about to take place.

The arms should pump several times before the take away.

Myth: **At the top of the backswing, the right hand should be positioned palm up, as if one were carrying a tray.**

Reality: **You are swinging a golf club, not serving hors d'oeuvres. Your right hand should be in a position that enables it to swing back to the ball.**

Diagram 1:
Right hand in the server's position.

Diagram 2:
The right hand is in a position of almost equal strength.

At the top of the backswing, the right hand should not be submissive to the left hand, but should offer some resistance to it. In Diagram 1 you see the right hand in a "giving- in," palms-up position. In Diagram 2 you can see the right hand in a position of almost equal strength. The proper cocking motion of the wrists creates the correct position of both hands. If you took the golf club and held it straight in front of you so your arms and the club were parallel with the ground, and then cocked your wrists vertically so the club was pointing straight to the sky, perpendicular to the ground, or in a ninety-degree relationship to your arms, this would be the correct hinging action of the wrists. Now if you turned your shoulders to the right and let the club position drop around parallel with the ground, you would have the correct hand position for the top of the backswing. You will notice in this position that the right hand is not in the "server's position" (palms up), but rather in an almost equal position with the left hand, with the palm of the right hand almost perpendicular to the ground. This position of the hand is very important because it affects the position of the club face. With the hands in the server's position, the club face is closed, making it almost impossible for the hands to release correctly on the downswing.

One reason women are told to use the server's position is that male-biased teaching methods tend to lump all women into one category: weak! When the right hand is in the server's position, it supports the club and left hand, which is why many pros tell women to use it. Granted, women do not possess the same amount of hand and forearm strength as men, but that does not mean that all women are of the same strength. I have seen women with excellent hand and forearm strength, as I have seen men who lack upper body strength. You see how the generalizations many golf pros employ in their teaching methods are wrong. The server's position is easy to teach. The golf pro just says, "Feel like you are carrying a tray in your right hand, and that is the correct position you want to be in at the top of your swing."

In all the golf lessons that I have given, I have never seen a woman who lacked the strength to execute the correct cocking action of the wrists on the backswing. The only way the server's position will be effective in the golf swing is if you combine it with a very strong leg drive. Since the right palm is facing the sky and making a closed club face, if the hands release correctly on the downswing, it will shut the club face, causing a topped shot. To avoid this it is necessary to have a very strong leg drive that will keep the club swinging down the target line without shutting down at impact. I would definitely not advise this for any amateur or even an experienced woman golfer. It requires far too much leg strength to be used effectively. Many male professionals who have played a closed club face have gotten away from it in their later years because of the amount of strength and timing it requires.

Another common reason women are taught the server's position is to correct a slice. Golf pros call this a Band-Aid technique. Band-Aid techniques are used when you give someone a quick fix in a lesson. You know that it will only work for that half-hour lesson or, if you're lucky, for one round of golf. After that, watch out. It is like putting a Band-Aid on a gushing wound. You stop the bleeding temporarily, but if the wound is too severe you know that no Band-Aid is going to work. Golf professionals often describe someone who has major swing problems as a "bleeder." I have often seen pros walking through the door shaking their heads and saying, "I've got a bleeder out there—someone call 911."

The Band-Aid in this situation is having the hands in the server's position with the club face closed. When the club swings back to the ball, the club face will be pointing to the left, thus making the ball go to the left. This is not really curing the slice. What it is doing is making you pull the ball to the left. If you continue to make this type of move, the situation will just get worse and worse. You will just be rehearsing the same outside-to-inside swing pattern. You must diagnose and work with the primary problem with the swing. There are no quick fixes in golf.

Myth of Keeping the Head Still

Left hand on center.

As I mentioned before, the "still head myth" is a dangerous one, which hampers the proper execution of the backswing. I cannot emphasize enough that trying to keep your head perfectly still with your eyes completely glued to the golf ball can cause many problems, particularly on the backswing. Never think about the head; think about the center. Put your left hand in the middle of your chest by your collarbone. This is the center for your upper body. Now with your hand on your chest, turn your shoulders to the right. When you turn, you will feel your center moving toward your right leg. Notice that your eyes will move to the right, behind the ball; they do not stay directly over it. This is the freedom that is necessary for the shoulders to turn correctly, for the weight to shift, and for all the components necessary for the execution of a proper backswing.

In sports such as baseball, hockey, and tennis, where a ball is in motion, watching the ball makes sense. But in golf, the ball is stationary, and even if you stare at it all day long, it is not going to move! So the last thing you want to worry about in your swing is looking at the ball and keeping the head still.

Myth of the Stiff Left Arm

In Chapter **1** on addressing the ball, we talked of how the arms should hang straight at the address. This straightness should not be created by tension but rather by gravity. In the backswing the left arm should remain extended from the body but *it should not be stiff!* There are two things you do not want the left arm to do on the backswing: You do not want it to remain perfectly straight because that would create tension, and you do not want it to break at the elbow (see illustration). There is, however, a happy compromise between the two, and that is bowing the left arm. When the arm is bowed, it bends slightly but does not break at the elbow.

Let me explain why not keeping the left arm stiff on the backswing is so important. You remember there are two things we want to accomplish when swinging the club back: the shoulders' turning and the wrists' cocking. *When you stiffen your arm, it is difficult for the wrists to cock.* Try putting a club in your hand and stiffening your left arm. Now swing the club back, letting the wrists cock. You will notice that it is very difficult for the wrists to do their work. Now relax both arms and swing the club back. It is much easier for the wrists to function correctly. Always remember that *tension is the golf swing's worst enemy.* You should never do anything to promote an inordinate amount of it. A stiff left arm also promotes the arms' swinging out away from the body on the backswing. Ideally we want the hands to stay the same distance from the body as they were at the address and not have them push straight back from the body. When the arm tenses, it will tend to push straight back away from the body, pushing the club on an outside swing path on the backswing.

Some golf professionals advocate actually breaking the left elbow at the top of the backswing. I have heard recently that some professionals are purporting it to be a new theory. However, I remember fifteen years ago in

Bent left arm.

Bowed left arm.

Florida several teaching professionals were dedicated to this idea. Their theory was that on the downswing, due to centrifugal force, the left arm will straighten back into its original position. They also believe that this adds an extra whipping effect into the golf swing, supplying greater club head speed. I experimented with this theory many years ago and I have witnessed others doing the same. My conclusion is that a bowed left arm at the top of the backswing is perfectly fine in most situations. However, as I stated before, a broken left arm is really not desired. I feel it adds too many movable parts, leaving additional problems to occur in a normal swing. But definitely do not try to force your left arm straight by tensing the muscles in it. If you are continuing to have a problem at the top of your swing with your left arm collapsing, try pushing the club away from your body with your right hand. Oftentimes it is not the left arm that is really the culprit, but rather the right arm is trying to dominate by pulling the club in closer to your body.

Myth of the Flying Elbow

On the backswing, when the wrists begin to cock it is perfectly natural for the right elbow to bend. *Do not try to control the elbow by tucking it into your side.* The right elbow will naturally move away from your body. Just because it is not tight at your side does not mean that it is flying. In regard to the right elbow, there are two things we do not want to do on the backswing: We do not want to keep the right elbow in by our side, and we do not want the tip of the elbow to point to the side or up in the air. I would much rather see the elbow fly a little than see it tucked into the side on the back swing. You have to realize that an incorrect move in the golf swing creates a domino effect. One bad move leads to another, which

Flying right elbow.

leads to another, and so on. For example, when you keep your elbow in at your side, this leads to a round-house take-away (wrapping the club around your body). This can lead to the hands' rolling (fanning the club), which leads to a reverse pivot, which causes the club to swing from the outside to the inside, which equals a *major slice*.

Myth: Lifting the Left Heel for Power

Women are commonly taught to lift the left heel on the backswing to generate power. Lifting the heel will not in itself give you more power. As a matter of fact, nine times out of ten you will lose power. Granted, you may hit one shot with some distance. But in order to do this everything must be perfectly timed when the left heel replants itself on the downswing.

You may see some golf professionals lift the left heel on the backswing. They are not consciously lifting the heel. The heel is being pulled up. These are two distinct motions. Many professional golfers started playing at a young age, and this pattern of lifting the heel may have started from the beginning or perhaps even later in their career. But the point is the heel is reacting to what the body is doing. The heel that is not adding to the body's movement. You will find that 99 percent of amateur golfers who lift the heel do so incorrectly. The heel is either being lifted intentionally or is being pulled up in response to a fault in their swing. I strongly recommend to all female golfers to keep the heel on the ground. Lifting it will cause nothing but trouble.

Myth: **At address, keep your right knee pointed in toward the middle of your stance to avoid swaying on your backswing.**

Fanning the club.

45

SPECIAL POINTER FOR WOMEN: *When you are out on the course and are playing a hole where you particularly want to hit a long ball, every bone in your body is going to want to twist up like a pretzel to try to send the ball soaring. You must learn to train yourself not to overdo your backswing and remember your backswing is for positioning, not for power.*

Reality: **Neither knee should be pointed toward the middle of your stance.**

At address, your weight should be distributed equally between the left and right feet. When in the address position, your knees should appear to be in alignment with your toes. The theory behind keeping the right knee pointing toward the middle of your stance is that it will keep you from swaying on your backswing. A sway occurs when instead of having your weight move to the right from your upper body's turning, it happens because your body leans toward the right. And kicking in your right leg will prevent this from happening. Unfortunately, this practice does not work. Instead, it forces your weight over to your left side at address, and on your backswing makes you sway to get the weight over toward your right foot. So you see that when you use this technique to stop a sway, you are in reality creating one.

• • •

4

The Top of the Backswing

••

The top of the backswing is a very crucial part of the full swing, for it will set the path for the downswing. The idea of the change of directions is literally what it means: You have swung in one direction and now you are going to swing in the opposite direction. This transition must be smooth and orderly. Think of when you breathe. The air does not just go in and out as quickly as possible, but rather comes in smoothly when you inhale and then reverses direction when you exhale. This reversing of direction when you breathe can be compared to the top of the backswing. You could even think of the swing as a sentence in which you insert a comma, as you continue on with your thought. The swing should not go "back-through," instead it should be "back and through" with a slight hesitation, giving you a chance to reverse your direction. This "and" that I am speaking of is really a pause at the top of your swing. If your mechanics are correct, this pause should happen naturally, but many times it does not. If you are a good-to-average golfer, it cannot hurt you to think of pausing before initiating the downswing.

When you swing the club back, it should be in a good position to swing forward through the ball. However, a golfer may have a less than picture-perfect backswing and somehow manage to get everything swinging on the correct path through the shot. This may work but it is really not desirable. Any time you get superfluous motion, it requires a great deal of timing and sometimes luck to get the club back to the ball. And when a swing with such motion does break down, it is not minimal. What once was a great shot now is literally topping the ball or hitting an inch behind it. So you can see we want the club's position to be the easiest for it to swing through the shot.

I have observed two different manners in which golf swings change directions. One is a rigid change of direction and the other is a flexible one. With the former, the hands are fully cocked by the time they reach the top of the backswing and are firmly set before they start their descent toward the ball. The latter occurs when the wrists do not fully cock on the backswing but actually cock on the downswing. The flexible change makes it feel as though the wrists are hinging and releasing at about the same time. The result is an incredible burst of almost effortless power. I have seen women with very little upper body strength who had a flexible change of direction smack the daylights out of the ball. The rigid change is usually found with women who are stronger in the hands and wrists. From the rigid change of direction, the arms, hands, and forearms lead firmly through the shot, resulting in a good clean shot.

The rigid change of direction is the most commonly taught manner in which to swing through. It is not complicated, and increasing one's physical strength will help to increase the distance the ball travels. The flexible change of direction is a little different. If solidly practiced and repeated, it is an awesome source of power, particularly for someone who lacks upper body strength. The only hitch to this is that it can border on being sloppy at the top of the backswing and actually lead to throwing the club head at the ball. The change of direction is crucial for the flexible swing. Since the wrists do not cock completely on the backswing but rather on the downswing, if the change of direction is not ideal, this can lead to the club's being thrown at the ball (see illustration). The rigid change of direction is better for the stronger hitter. The flexible change of direction is more common to see with the swinger. Hitters use more bodily strength when swinging the club, and swingers (the majority of women) use timing and employ more physics to generate their power.

You should not worry about whether you are a hitter or a swinger. Just be aware that the top of the backswing is an important place of change. Always try to get a feel for where the top of your backswing is. Many people do not even feel when the backswing has wound down or come to a completion. It is important at first to feel the distinction between backswing and downswing.

Another crucial element in the change of direction is your weight shift. Once your arms and hands have begun to return on the same path that they took on the backswing, your weight will begin to shift to your left side. This timing is crucial. At this point your lower body should not transfer your weight too quickly, leaving the hands and arms behind, but rather the lower body should shift the weight in response to the upper body's movement. If the weight transfer were too slow, this might promote a casting motion. So you can see this change of direction at the top of the swing is going to be very important. Let's take an example of someone who has swung the club back too far on her backswing. This now will throw the body off on the downswing because instead of having the club in the correct position, it is pointing toward the ground. And instead of having the weight on the right foot she is probably leaning slightly toward her left side, putting her in a reverse pivot (see Chapter 11 on troubleshooting). This puts her transition state (change of direction) in trouble. She will now somehow manage to compensate by getting the arms and hands into the correct position on her backswing. And

**Wrists prematurely uncocking—
"throwing the club head."**

since her weight is already on the left side, it will be impossible for her to make the proper weight shift when returning through to the ball. This is where the idea of balance and symmetry (see Chapter 3 on balance and symmetry) is so important in the swing. At the top of your swing, you want to be balanced and poised to make the correct downswing. You might want to liken the top of the backswing to an automobile engine. Your engine runs smoothly when all of the pistons fire in the correct order. But if one starts misfiring, it is time for a tune-up, or else you will be in for a rough ride!

When first learning golf, your timing at the top of your swing will be awkward. You will have to consciously think of making a pause and probably consciously try to shift your weight from the right foot to the left on the downswing. However, as we have discussed in earlier chapters, it's best to take the golf swing from being a consciously performed act and make it an unconscious reaction. So at first it may be awkward, but as time goes by your body learns to make this transition instinctively. For this to happen, all the variables at the top of your swing (position of the wrists, where the shaft of the club points, height of the hands, amount of shoulder turn, and posture) must be the same, or as consistent as possible, every time you swing the club back. This goes back to the idea that the backswing is for position, not for power. Get the club in the same position every time so that your body can learn to begin the downswing in the same manner every time. This is why golf requires so much practice, because the repetition of positioning is so important. Once your body learns how it must come through the ball, it will be able to automatically compensate for minor errors that occur on the backswing. But first you need to learn to swing the club back into position before you can learn to swing the club through.

Let me give you an example of what I am talking about. Let's say you have swung the back a little outside of your normal backswing line. If you were a beginner to even intermediate player, chances are you would return on your downswing on that same path. This outside to inside swing would, of course, produce a pull or a slice. So being out of position at the top of your backswing produces a bad shot. Let's say you were a professional golfer and you made the same error. After hitting so many golf balls and having acquired a feel for the correct positioning on the downswing, it is quite possible that unconsciously your body will make an adjustment to put the club on the correct path. On her downswing, the professional golfer might unconsciously drive the legs a little stronger than normal, which might lower the arms and hands onto the correct path, which would result in an excellent shot even though she was out of position at the top of her swing. It is this muscle memory of the subconscious that knows what position the club should be in at impact and will try to do everything it can to make that happen.

Perhaps you have felt this in your own swing. Maybe you have felt your legs jumping far ahead of your upper body on your downswing. There can be several reasons for this, but after a process of elimination, you might find that the reason this is happening is that you are out of position at the top of your backswing. Unconsciously your body is trying to put the club on the correct swing path by forcing your legs far ahead in an attempt to lower your arms. Let's say that on your downswing you have slightly cast the club head. Your body might compensate for this by pulling up slightly out of your posture, enabling the club face to square up to the golf ball. You might hear a professional say after playing a tournament, "I was just barely getting back to the ball. I was scrambling the whole day." What she is saying is that something was wrong with her swing and her subconscious, in trying to adjust for this error, made her swing feel awkward and as though she were just barely returning to the ball (even though she may have shot a 70 for the day's round). So you see, you do not have to have the club in perfect position at the top of your backswing every time. If you are experienced enough, it is very possible for you to recover on your downswing. However, if you are a beginning to intermediate player who only gets out to play and practice a few times a week, you are asking an awful lot expecting to get the club into the correct position on the downswing.

Exercise: This is a good practice exercise to get a feel for where the top of your backswing occurs. Looking into a mirror, take your pitching wedge and swing the club back halfway (about hip high). Now swing the club back three quarters (about chest level) and then make a full swing (with the shaft of the club parallel to the ground). Get a feeling for these three different positions, particularly the top of the backswing.

Now go to a driving range. Hit balls with a half-swing, then three-quarter swing, then full swing. It is important that you know where your hands are at all times in relation to your body.

5

The Downswing

The downswing is basically a reversal of the backswing. Assuming you have swung the club back correctly, you will now want to swing through in the same correct manner. As in the backswing, the downswing involves a succession of events. These events are designed to deliver the club face squarely back to the ball and through, toward your target.

This is the part of the golf swing where everything has to come together. Ideally, when you start your downswing the club is in perfect position and ready to attack the ball. The downswing should be the complete opposite of the backswing. At the top of your backswing, your chest is in a straight line with your right leg. At the conclusion of your downswing, your upper body will have completed its full 180- degree rotation and your chest will be in a straight line with your left leg. This upper body rotation is the basic idea of the swing. You have simply turned to your right and then turned back through toward your left. On your backswing the weight shifted onto your right foot. On the downswing the weight will now move over to your left foot. The entire time this is happening your body will be tilted in the same posture it was at your address. At no point in the swing do you want to intentionally straighten your spinal column (stand erect).

The arms and hands should be swinging with the shaft of the club, not throwing the club head at the ball. This is the basic motion that you want for the downswing. Now let's go into greater detail.

What Starts the Downswing?

Three motions happen simultaneously:

1. Your upper body begins to uncoil.
2. Your arms return on the same path that they took on the backswing.
3. The weight shifts from your right to left foot.

To simplify this, all you should think of when swinging the club forward is to let the arms return on the same arc that they created on the backswing. This in itself will force the other two motions to occur.

When the downswing starts, everyone seems to experience a different sensation in regard to what part of their anatomy is moving first. Some may say they feel their weight shifting to the left; others may say it is the hips' uncoiling, others the hands dropping back through the target line. All these feelings are valid because these three motions happen almost simultaneously. However, the weight shifting and the hips' unwinding should occur in anticipation of the forearms swinging and the upper body uncoiling. Ideally, at the top of your backswing the hips have turned forty-five degrees, and the shoulders ninety. As the upper body

Downswing

unwinds it is trying to catch up to the hips. Since the hips have turned only forty-five degrees and the shoulders ninety, the arms and hands are going to have to move quickly in an attempt to catch the hips. They never quite do, but the closer they come, the more power is generated. Try to visualize the top of your swing. Now if you want the club to return on the same path that it took on the backswing, the hips must get out of the way. This movement is not a jerky movement but a response to the arms swinging.

Also try to sense what is happening to your weight. It has to move to the left foot to enable the arms to return on their original path. If your arms and hands are moving through the shot but your body is not leading, the only choice you have is to take the wrists and whip the club head through. However, with your weight shifting, you are able to maintain your original backswing position longer on your downswing. As your weight is shifting, you should remain in the posture that you established at your address. Your eyes should be focused toward the ball but not staring directly at it. After you have hit the ball, you will begin to assume the opposite position that you had on the backswing. For example, if you were to stand directly behind someone (say it's a woman), you would notice that on her backswing the club face would be pointing toward the right. And if you watched her downswing, you would see that once the club had made contact with the ball, it would now point left of the target line. After the club had swung as far as possible from her body on the follow-through the wrists, as with the backswing, would cock again, bringing the club back toward her body.

Put your left hand slightly below your collarbone. This is your upper body's center. It is simply turning from the right to the left. As this center is turning, it is increasing in velocity, trying to catch up with the hips. The arms and hands are swinging, increasing in their velocity, trying to catch the center. And ideally, the club head is lagging behind the arms and hands, and eventually will catch up to them at impact at an even greater rate of speed. Once the club has swung through, the hips should now be pointing forty-five degrees left of their original address position. Leaving your upper body's center pointing toward your target, you should now be looking at the flight of your ball. You should have maintained your posture through impact, but if you like, you may now stand erect since the ball has already been hit. Your weight should be completely on your left side, and your hands and arms should be in complete control of the club's shaft. How high or low your hands finish will in part be determined by your backswing. If your backswing is upright (with hands positioned high), your follow-through will also be high. As I stated earlier, the down-swing is reversing the process of what happened on the backswing. When all parts of your body move correctly on the downswing, the club should be in the same posi-tion at impact that it was at address.

> *Myth:* **Keep the club face pointing down the target line on your downswing.**
> *Reality:* **The club face should point in the opposite direction of where it pointed on the backswing.**

The toe of the club points toward the sky when swinging back; it should also point toward the sky when you follow through. Do not try to make the club face point toward your target at impact. If you do this, you will actually lose acceleration and, worse yet, even shank the ball.

> *Myth:* **The downswing is initiated and controlled by the lower body.**
> *Reality:* **The lower body should be responding to the upper body's movements.**

As the arms swing through toward your target, your weight will shift to the left foot. You do not want to force your weight over to the left. Simply let it get pulled over by the swinging arms.

Every move that we make in the golf swing is a move that is designed to maintain the angle formed by the cocked wrists as long as possible on the downswing. You should feel the arms make the initial move on the downswing. This part can get a little tricky because you do not want to intentionally uncock the wrists, yet at the same time, you do not want to keep that angle too long.If you ever take practice swings trying to consciously keep that angle, always swing through. Do not practice keeping that angle until impact and stop. Usually what happens when you try to maintain that angle for too long is that the ball either goes to the right or you start shanking the ball. Neither is desired. The best thing to do is to simply be aware that the arms lead on the downswing, and try to keep the hands from throwing the club head toward the ball at the top of your swing.

> *Myth:* **On the downswing the hips and legs are solely responsible for power in the golf swing.**
> *Reality:* **It is the relationship of the body's movement to the swinging and maintaining of the angle formed by the cocked wrists that creates power.**

The source of power in the golf swing is the same for men as for women. Unfortunately, golf professionals often tell women to use various parts of their body to generate power. If women do so, they actually lose power. For instance, women are often taught to throw their hips into the swing. This *inhibits* club head speed and does not enhance it. When swinging the club back, the wrists cock and form a ninety-degree angle. It is the delay of the release of this angle on the downswing that creates power. In other words, the club head lags behind the hands, maintaining this angle as long as possible before releasing at impact with the ball. This is the source of power. Every movement that we make in the golf swing should be a movement that helps to maintain this angle.

Once the wrists have cocked at the top of the backswing, and the downswing has been initiated, the body must move out of the way to enable the hands to maintain their angle and swing at maximum speed. If the body moves too quickly and gets too far in front of the hands, this will cause an early release of the angle and a subsequent loss of power. If the body does not get out of the way of the hands' swinging, this also will cause an early release with the same results.

So you can see that the swing has to be harmoniously timed between the speed of the hands the body's movement. Again, no part of the body is solely responsible for power. It is the timing of the weight shift and the hands' swinging that helps maintain the angle and subsequent release of power.

> *Myth:* **Slow the speed of your downswing.**
> *Reality:* **You are swinging the club. Do not**
> **direct on the downswing.**

Where most women get into trouble is when they try to guide the club to the ball. A golf swing is not a forced or contrived movement. When you try to make it so, the results are disastrous. The necessary element in the downswing is the element of acceleration. The arms, hands, and body should be increasing in their speed, never decreasing in their momentum. If one of these links falters, you will experience a domino effect. Let's say your weight does not shift quickly enough. This in turn will make the arms lose their acceleration, which will force the hands to slow down, which will lead to club head throw-away (casting), which will usually result in a shot you *wish* you could forget. (Throwing the club head is golf lingo for uncocking the wrists prematurely on the downswing.) Your intention on the downswing is to maintain acceleration through the shot. (Sounds easy, right?) Understanding the idea of acceleration is important because it will help you execute the downswing correctly.

When I speak of acceleration, I do not mean consciously taking the club and trying to make the club head itself move quickly by throwing it at the ball. What I am speaking of is a chain reaction where all the parts move efficiently together. Everything we do in the golf swing is designed to maintain the angle formed by the wrist cock on the downswing as long as possible. To do this our first move on the downswing should be to shift the weight from the right foot over to the left foot. It is simple logic: Our weight should shift toward our target as we are hitting the ball. If you were throwing a ball, you wouldn't shift your weight backward to throw the ball forward. You would put your weight and momentum in the direction you wanted the ball to go. This weight shift should start the chain reaction of the downswing. Once the weight has shifted, your arms and hands are free to swing to the ball. Do not try to guide the club to the ball. Just let your arms drop back to the ball the same way they swung from the ball. All you should be doing is reversing what was done on the backswing.

Generating Power

Myth: Women are not anatomically designed for golf.

Reality: Due to the physical makeup of the average woman, women have a greater ability for golf than men. Women have an innate sense of generating power that is conducive to the golf swing. Ladies, you are natural golfers! If anyone ever tells you that women are not designed for golf, stop them dead in their tracks.

It is normal when performing an athletic feat for the mind to subconsciously want to use the strongest part of the body. For example, if you had a piece of wood in your hands—let's say, a two-by-four—and there was a ball on a tee that you wanted to hit far, how would you hit it? If you were a man, your tendency would be to generate power with your hands, forearms, and shoulders, slashing at the ball. This is normal because *most men have a great deal of upper body strength*. However, for a woman lacking upper body strength, there is a subconscious effort to use the whole body to generate power, almost a natural sense of timing where the legs, torso, and hands work together to generate power. *This is precisely what is necessary in the golf swing.* I have often marveled at how some women, never having played another sport, pick up a golf club and swing it with such ease. Even a very uncoordinated woman will take to golf easily if taught properly. Many women tell me at our first lesson, "I have no coordination; I'm terrible at sports. Please just get me to hit the ball." What they do not realize is that even if what they say is true, they swing the club better than twice the men who have the same abilities. When people lack athletic ability, there is even a greater tendency to rely on their natural inclinations. For example, a man with little athletic ability will be strongly inclined to use his hands and forearms to hit the ball (which is what we do not want). A woman with the same ability will have a tendency to use too much body motion. Using too much body motion can always be toned down to create a smooth, effective swing. However, a man with a tendency to slash at the ball is another story. This is not an easy cure.

Besides the fact that women have a natural propensity for the game, I believe that, in general, they are much easier to teach than men. As I stated earlier, many women assume the attitude that they are not very good and need to learn. On the other hand, men will very rarely admit that their coordination is not all that good. Their attitude normally is that they are good athletes, "it's just that this damn game of golf is so confounding."

Another factor that holds men back is their desire to hit the ball far. When a foursome of men play golf together, the player who hits a long ball is held in high esteem (even if it goes into the woods). So men put added pressure on themselves to hit the ball farther. When they do this, there is undue pressure on their swing, and chances are it will break down during a round of golf. Even when I teach men during a lesson, I have to keep repeating, "Do not try to hit the ball far." It usually takes about three or four lessons before they realize that I am interested in how they are swinging the club, not in how far the ball is going.

> *Myth:* If you just put your hips into the shot, that ball will *really* go far!
>
> *Reality:* The hips are not directly responsible for power in the golf swing.

Do not make turning your hips the first move on your downswing. As the weight moves to the left side, the hips will naturally unwind. The hips should never get too far ahead of the upper body. When this happens what we call a spinout will occur. This means your body has literally spun around (see illustration) and usually results in a shot that goes dead to the right or that goes dead to the left. Either way, this is not what we want. The power does not come from having the hips release much faster than the upper body but from having the upper body try to catch up to the hips. The upper body never does actually catch up to the hips at impact but it should definitely be closing in on them.

Hips "spinning out."

> *Myth:* **For extra distance, drive those legs into the shot.**
>
> *Reality:* **The legs should simply react to the upper body uncoiling. They are not solely responsible for power in the golf swing.**

Yes, you do use your legs on the downswing, but their role is to transfer your weight and set your body in motion toward the ball. However, using a greater leg drive will not increase the length of your shot. The swing is a harmoniously integrated event, with no one part of the body being responsible for distance. If the legs move too quickly on the downswing, they will get too far ahead of the rest of the body and cause a loss of acceleration.

> *Myth:* **On the downswing, try to swing from the inside to the outside.**
>
> *Reality:* **Let the club return to the ball. Do not manipulate its path.**

The golf swing should be a natural movement, not a contrived one. When you get to the top of your backswing, if you can say to yourself, "OK, now I'm gonna swing this club from the inside to outside," *you are already in big trouble*. You should never have enough time to think that much. If you do, you are no longer swinging the club but rather thinking the club through the swing. This is a big no-no! I can't tell you how many problems the thought of swinging from the inside to the outside has caused for professionals and amateurs alike. People who are afraid of swinging outside to inside do anything they can just to get that inside path. Relax! Coming a little over the top of the ball (outside to inside) is not terrible. I would much rather see that than have someone consciously try to swing the club from the inside. A common swing thought is to tuck the right elbow in at one's side during the downswing to get that inside position. If this is your swing thought, the chances are nine out of ten that it is creating a problem in your swing. Invariably women who practice this inside-to-outside swing end up dropping their right shoulder on the downswing and hitting behind the ball. Or they come so far from the inside that they push the ball to the right. In this case the hips and shoulders do not turn correctly and end up sliding to the right trying to keep that doggone club coming from the inside. Forget all this "inside path" business and concentrate more on a rhythmic pattern of swinging, and I guarantee golf will be a lot more enjoyable.

When you swing the club back correctly, it is already on the inside path. When you turn in the opposite direction, coming back to the ball, it is going to move from the inside. There are reasons that can force the club to the outside, but even then it is really nothing terrible to come over the ball a little. So, if you stop worrying about having your downswing on the

Club is being forced from the inside to outside the target line, which will result in a pushed shot.

correct path, you will hit the ball better than when you were guiding the club.

> *Myth:* **Try to hit down and under the ball to take a divot.**
> *Reality:* **Never intentionally hit down or under.**

Have you ever heard professional golfers describe a shot where they intentionally hit down and tried to get under the ball? Probably so, but in reality this is not what they did. When golf professionals think of getting "under the ball," they will make a swing that will be entirely different than that of an amateur who has the same concept. When seasoned professionals think of hitting down on a ball to get a desired effect, they do not literally hit down on it with the club head. Over the years they have learned the correct manner in which to get a descending blow on the ball. When you tell amateurs to try to get under the ball, they will end up throwing the club head and lifting the body out of position. Whenever the club makes contact with the ball, it does not lift it into the air. The ball gets its lift from the loft of the club. That is why you have clubs with different lofts and shaft lengths. When you desire a different shot you should simply change clubs, not your technique. Sometimes a golfer will try to hit down on the ball to take a divot. If this is the case, there can be several reasons why he or she is not taking a divot. But attempting to make a divot by throwing the club head into the ground will just make the situation worse.

> *Myth:* **Stay behind the ball until after impact.**
> *Reality:* **On the downswing, the momentum of your swing should pull you to your left side.**

Left hand on center.

Never stay behind the ball through impact. Your body, arms, and hands should have such momentum that they pull you through the shot. What is so devastating about staying behind the ball is that, as we have discussed, acceleration is a very important part of the downswing. Think about it: If your arms, hands, and club are accelerating but you are keeping your body behind the ball, it is rather like running into a brick wall. Keeping one part of the anatomy still will force the other parts to lose their acceleration. When that happens, the cause is lost. The shot can go anywhere and usually does. Let your body release through the shot. I am not advocating moving yourself ahead of the ball at impact, but don't force yourself behind the ball. It is really a nasty habit to break. You might want to think of your body as centered somewhere close to the ball at impact. Put your left hand in the center of your chest above your breasts. Think of this as your center and have this center somewhere near the ball at impact.

Remember the idea of the downswing is to maintain the angle as long as possible. Do not try to do this consciously; just know that this is supposed to happen. If you obsess on this move, you will probably end up shanking the ball or blocking the shot out (not releasing the hands).

Power in a Woman's Swing

Three factors determine the distance the ball will travel: club head speed, swing path, and the portion of the club that makes contact with the ball. It is my belief that women have been so poorly taught about what generates and how to generate power in their swings that they will inevitably hit the ball a short distance. Most women are capable of hitting the ball 10 to 15 yards farther than their current distance. For example, a woman who has been told to throw her hips into the shot will not gain distance in nine out of ten golf swings. The problem is that every once in a while she will hit a long ball and immediately assume that what is necessary is to put even more hips into the shot.

You have to realize that once you put your hips, legs, or other part of your anatomy into a shot, you are probably throwing off one of the factors that give you distance. For example, if you throw your hips, chances are you will cast the club head, which leads to a loss of club head speed. It also changes the path and position where the club head will make contact with the ball. You will get our power from the rotation of the upper body coupled with swinging the hands and not throwing the club head.

A Woman's Efficiency Ratio

Granted, the average male has more upper body strength than the average female. However, when you watch an average male swing a golf club, you will also see that the efficiency of his swing is very low. By efficiency I mean the innate power that a man possesses and the actual output of the swing. For instance, if you watch a muscle-bound twenty-two-year-old male hit a ball, you will see that his natural swing will probably misdirect or misuse 50 percent of his power. So his ratio would be high physical output with a low result. If you watch an average middle-aged woman hit a ball, the ratio of her physical output and resultant hit will be much closer. In other words, even though the woman is not as strong as the man, her swing is more efficient, so she gets more out of the shot.

When the twenty-two-year-old male does make contact with the ball, you can be assured that it will go soaring but his level of consistency will be very poor. Our middle-aged woman's shot may never soar, but she will be much more consistent with her results. I have seen women who seemed to lack any type of physical strength whack the daylights out of the ball. When I say whack the daylights it may mean that the ball goes 150 yards. But when you watch women swing, every ounce of energy and all body movements work so efficiently together that they have used all their physical energy in the most productive manner. When you take our body-building twenty-two-year-old, with his strength, the ball should go 300 yards, but in reality it is only going 180. So again we would say that his input is much higher than his output, making for a very low efficiency ratio. Most male golf pros turn up their noses at an elderly woman hitting a drive 150 yards, thinking she can't hit the ball when the reality of the situation is that if you took her physical strength into consideration, she smacks the daylights out of the ball. I have worked with older men with much more upper body strength who only hit the ball 150 yards. So you see, hitting the ball a long distance does not mean you have a good or efficient swing, or that it will go straight. It just means that you muscled the ball out there, and muscle does not make a golf swing. If you do not believe me, go sit on the first tee of any golf course and take note of the results. As a woman once said to me, "I don't enjoy playing golf with men." As she paused, I thought she would reply, "because they always criticize my swing," but she then smiled at me and added, "They're *always* in the woods!"

6

The Finish

One should not have to force a correct finish. If the downswing is good, the finish will be correct.

If you make a correct backswing and a correct downswing, you will have a correct finish. But sometimes thinking about how you should finish will force your backswing and downswing to work in the right manner.

Our primary concern on the follow-through is that the angle the spine creates at address be maintained throughout the swing. In other words, once you have bent from the hips you should stay bent. You do not want your body to straighten out during the downswing and subsequent follow-through. The follow-through should be similar to the backswing, only in the opposite direction. For example, if you will remember, on the backswing the shoulders should be turned and the wrists should be cocked. The same holds true for the follow-through. Not only will your shoulders be completely turned (see illustration on page 70), but the wrists will cock just as they did on the backswing. You will also notice in the illustration that the toe of the club points toward the sky about

Toe of the club points toward the sky on the backswing.

halfway back on the backswing, and the toe of the club is also pointing toward the sky about halfway up on the follow-through. From this point the wrists should take the initial shock of pulling the club back toward the body by breaking or cocking. Once this happens then the arms can fold. For the correct follow-through, the shoulders should be completely rotated, and all your weight should have been pulled over to your left foot by the arms' swinging. You must always remember that the golf swing really moves from the right to the left, and it should do so in a very level fashion.

Myth: **Finish high and let it fly.**
Reality: **You should stay in the posture that you assumed at address as much as possible.**

Toe of the club points toward the sky on the follow-through.

The only time you should finish with your hands high in the air is if your backswing is very upright. As was previously stated, the downswing is just a reversal of the backswing. So if your arc was steep on the backswing, it should be steep on the follow-through. Forcing yourself to finish with your hands high does nothing but ensure an occasional top or whiffed shot.

If you put your left hand on the center of your chest covering your collarbone, you will locate the center of your upper body. In the golf swing the arms should try to catch up to this center on the downswing. The center should not get far ahead of the arms and club head (see illustration). Generally speaking, that's exactly what will happen if you intentionally try to finish with your hands high in the air. You will create a whipping effect in which the center leads on the downswing and accelerates far more quickly than the arms and hands—the whipping effect in which the hands end up finishing very high.

Center is too far ahead of the arms and club head on downswing.

Myth: Feel the club head hit your back on the follow-through.

Reality: Your follow-through should be as controlled as your backswing. You should never lose so much control that the club hits you in the back.

Usually when the club hits your back, it is for the previously mentioned reason that the center has gotten far ahead of the hands and shaft of the club or that instead of letting the wrists bend first on the follow-through, the arms have bent first. You must remember that the wrists take the initial shock of pulling the club in on the follow-through, not the arms.

Myth: Make sure that your stomach is facing the target on the follow-through.

Reality: Your arms pull your body through. Do not intentionally force yourself into this position.

Remember, you are swinging from the right to the left. Do not swing around your body (horizontally) on the backswing or downswing.

Here's one more note on the follow-through. Ideally the golf swing is a very relaxed, balanced, level motion. When you have completed your swing, you should hold your finish and keep yourself in balance. Here are a few check points to review while you hold your finish:

1. Make sure your weight is completely on the left foot.
2. Your spine should be much at the same angle that it was at address.
3. You should have complete control of the shaft and club head at your finish.

4. Your center should be facing toward your target since the shoulders have completely rotated:

Myth: **Finish with your back arched in the position of a reversed letter *c*.**
Reality: **You should finish with your spine straight—not arched backward.**

A teaching practice or belief common about fifteen years ago was that when you finished your swing your back should be arched, forming a reversed letter *c*. I sincerely hope this type of finish is not being taught anywhere, because it is severely outdated, and potentially harmful to your back. When I was in college, this was commonly believed to be the best way to finish a golf swing. I can only guess how many potentially great golfers ruined their backs trying to emulate this finish. Because of the damage this method has done, I do not believe any competent professional today is still teaching it. On very rare occasions golfers will come to me trying to finish in this manner. Usually it is because they put their clubs away fifteen years ago and are just starting to play again, and are not aware of the changes in swing theory. If you make a correct golf swing, there should never be any undue pressure or strain on your back, particularly the lower back. The theory behind the reverse *c* was that you wanted to finish in this position to ensure that you had stayed behind the ball at impact. If you notice, in this type of finish what causes the *c* is that your head is slanting backward.

Not only did this finish cause a variety of lower back problems, it also caused some severe swing problems. Any time your head stays still and your body arches backward, the hands will tend to whip through, resulting in a pull hook. I have watched aspiring professional golfers who assumed this finish struggle terribly with a hook that seemed to appear when the pressure was the most intense. The upper body must always release through the shot. This release is not only a source of power but it keeps the club head moving along the target line for the hands to whip through and pull across your body. This incorrect finish was taught to men and women, but women were targeted more, because of their flexibility. Most men, used to sports such as football and weight lifting, have short, stubby muscles across their upper body that are not conducive to flexibility. Most women, on the other hand, have long, smooth, striated muscles in their upper bodies, which lends them more flexibility than these men. It is exactly because of this flexibility that many women were told to make a nice arch in their swing and, upon making such a finish, were lauded for having a beautiful swing. Such a position may look good, but leave it for gymnastics. When it comes to golf, an erect finish is what is desired for both men and women.

7

The Practice Swing

Myth: **During the practice swing, pick a spot and try to hit it as if it were a golf ball.**

Reality: **By picking a spot to hit, you are rehearsing the wrong movements in the golf swing.**

You often hear people say, "If I could just bottle that practice swing and use it every time a ball is there, I would be on the tour." However, no one seems to want to analyze what the difference is between their regular swing and their practice swing. The difference is simple: A ball is there! When you are swinging the club without a ball, you are more than likely really *swinging* the club. Once you put a ball there, the swinging motion tends to become a contrived motion. In other words, you end up trying to direct the club head toward the ball rather than just swinging on a path. When a person is swinging freely, everything should feel light and natural. When you stare at the golf ball with the intention of getting it in the air, it is a different story. You start using all the wrong muscles to try to lift the ball and make it go far! Both conscious intentions can be extremely destructive to a good golf swing.

When you take a practice swing, your point of focus should not be picking a spot and trying to hit it, but rather thinking about what is going on in your backswing and downswing. Any time people pick a spot at which to aim, they tend to pick a very small area (usually a quarter of the size of a golf ball), and their main intent is to deliver the club right back to that point. All this is doing is setting them up to rehearse the wrong motions. I often ask people on the practice tee what they are swinging at, and they often say, "Oh, just that spot right there." When I ask them to show me the spot, usually it is just a small point not nearly the size of a golf ball.

What is worse is that most of them will try to keep their head over that spot. When you ask someone where their head is, they will point with one finger toward their forehead and say, "This is my head!" In fact, the head is much bigger than just a point, and a golf ball will take up far more space than a speck on the ground. The idea that I am getting at is, do not think about spots or points but think on a grander scale. Think of the wholeness of the swinging motion, such as of the weight shifting and hands swinging. Do not try to force the club head to hit a particular point. Although you should not be aiming at a specific point, you should let the club make contact with the ground. Never take a practice swing without allowing your arms to extend fully through the downswing. If they do extend fully, you will graze the grass or take a divot. Another important rule to remember is never to stop on your downswing at the bottom of your arc or impact position; always swing through. If you stop at impact position enough times on your practice swing, you can be fairly certain that on your real swing you will start shanking or slicing the ball.

A very important part of the practice swing is the grip. Whenever you start your practice swing, your hands exert a certain amount of initial pressure on the club. After several practice swings, release the hands and regrip. The pressure that was in the initial setup and the pressure that exists after several practice swings are dramatically different. Every time you swing the club through to your finish, your grip pressure increases. Without releasing this pressure, tension increases dramatically. You must think of the hands as acting as a pressure valve. After every practice swing you must let go of the club to release the pressure. If you do not let go of the club after each swing, you are asking for serious trouble, even the possibility of whiffing the ball. As your hand pressure increases after each swing (assuming you do not release the hands) so does the tension in your forearms and shoulders. All this tension can lead to disastrous result. As you will recall from previous chapters, stiffness and tension inhibit the swinging motion. When you have tension to that degree you are no longer creating a swinging motion. You then have a contrived motion, in which everything is forced and nothing happens naturally.

8

The Short Game

The short game usually refers to any shot attempted within 60 yards of the green. Included in the short game are chipping, pitching, putting, and the sand game.

Chipping

Chipping is a stroke that involves a short backswing and follow-through. Usually the goal when chipping is not to loft the ball much. Instead you want to obtain just enough loft and speed to land the ball on the green, enabling it to roll into the hole.

The main thing to remember when learning the short game is that it relies on a sense of touch, or finesse, more than on any other aspect of the swing. What I mean by touch is the ability to gauge the power you need to employ when 50 yards or closer to the green.

If you think about it, the full swing is really quite easy. You make the same full-shoulder turn every time, and ideally the club should be in the same position at the top of your backswing. In the short game this is not going to be the case. What is going to determine the distance the ball will travel is how much of a backswing you take. For example, if I am 20 yards from the green, I do not want to take a full backswing because that would result in the ball's traveling the maximum distance the club would allow. So now I must try to decide how far to swing the club back for a 20-yard shot. *This is not easily done!* It takes time before you can train your body to sense the correct amount of back-swing for the desired distance. To learn distances and how much of a backswing to take you must employ all your senses. There are a few mechanical fundamentals to be used but the rest should be all your touch or feel. This finesse is acquired through much experience and practice.

> *Myth:* **When making a chip shot, move your arms, hands, and shoulders like a pendulum.**
>
> *Reality:* **By forcing your upper body to function as a pendulum, you are practicing the wrong motions to execute a good chip shot.**

When you think of a pendulum, you think of a rigid mechanical movement—just the opposite of the motion you should use on a chip shot. The only way to achieve a sense of the feel on the chip shot is to think more about the hands swinging, rather than a rigid posture. There should be very little body motion. The first thing to do is to bend from the hips with the arms hanging vertically. By doing this you are segmenting your body. For example, bending from the hip joint segments the upper body from the lower body, enabling the upper body to have freedom of movement from the lower body. Hanging the arms vertically creates a forty-five-degree angle. The difference between the vertical hang of the arms and the angled shaft of the club creates another segmentation, which allows the arms and hands to swing free of the body from a precocked position (see illustration).

You will notice the arms and hands are not in perfectly straight alignment with the club. Rather, the arms hang straight and the shaft of the club is angled at about forty-five degrees. If your arms were in straight alignment with the club (looking like a pendulum), this would promote the use of the large muscles of the body. However, with the arms hanging straight and the shaft of the club being angled, this segmentation helps the smaller muscles of the body take control and, by doing so, enables you to incorporate finesse into the shot.

You want to position the ball so it is in the middle of your feet or slightly left of center. The feet should be fairly close together—maybe 12 inches apart. You want the feet in this position because putting them close together sends a unconscious message to the brain that you do not need a great deal of balance because you are going to be making a delicate, light shot.

On this shot many players like to open their stance. By opening the stance I mean that the feet and shoulders are pointing slightly left of the target. In other words, you open your body toward the target. You do not have to do this, but some players feel that they can see the target better by doing so.

Now you're set to swing the club. Remember, the factor that determines the distance the ball will travel is how much of a backswing you take. If you want the ball to go a short distance, take a short backswing. The amount of your backswing is also going to dictate the amount of your follow-through. If it is swung back 8 inches, then you must swing through 8 inches. When you are swinging the club back and through, make sure the

Shaft of club is at a 45-degree angle to the arms.

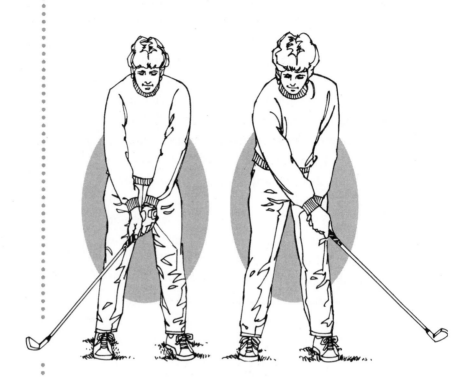

Wrists swinging the club head.

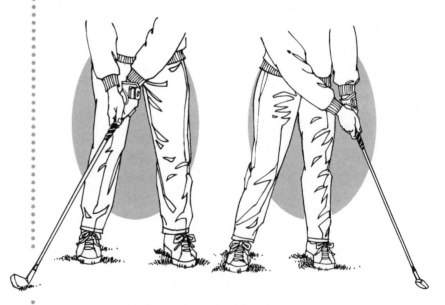

Hands moving with the club head.

club head swings with your hands rather than having your hands swing the club head (see illustration). If you notice your wrists breaking and feel that they are swinging the club, you could be in trouble. If you remember in Chapter 1 on the address, when you set up to the ball you want to form the letter Y, only the stem of the Y is going to be tilted at a forty-five-degree angle.

On the chip shot keep this Y together. You do not want it turning into a Z. When you keep this Y together the stem of the Y (being the shaft of the club) should move, with your hands and arms forming the upper part of the Y. The shoulders will make a turn to the right on the backswing. The amount that they will turn will, of course, depend on how much of a backswing you are taking. But the main thing here is not to worry too much about the shoulders. Just make sure the hands and club head are moving together.

> *Myth:* **When swinging through on a chip shot, keep the club face pointing toward your target.**
>
> *Reality:* **This should be done only for specialty shots. If this is done on a regular chip, it could lead to shanking the ball.**

The toe of the club on your backswing should be pointing toward the sky, and the same is true for the follow-through. Make sure that you do not try to accomplish this position by rolling the hands over on the backswing (fanning the club face) or on your follow-through. It is the shoulders' turning that opens the club on the backswing. If you try to keep the club square toward the target through impact, it will force your right shoulder to drop and your body to pull up on the follow-through. You want to swing from the right to the left sides of your body—not under and up. On your follow-through you should feel your weight being pulled over to the left side. Again, as with the full swing, you are tilted from the hips at address. You should keep this posture on the follow-through.

> *Myth:* **Putt, do not chip, whenever possible.**
> *Reality:* **Use whichever club you feel most comfortable with.**

If your ball is located on the frog hair (the finely mowed area just off the green), you will be faced with several options. One is, Should I putt or chip? The other is, Should I leave the flagstick (pin) in the hole or remove it? To answer the first question, use whatever club you feel more confident with. I am sure you have heard that you should always roll the ball if you can because this leaves a greater margin for error. The only problem with this theory is that putting may not be a strong part of your game. If you feel more comfortable using an iron rather than a putter, than go ahead and use it. As to the question of whether or not to leave the flagstick in the hole, there are two different theories. One is that without the flagstick, the hole is bigger; therefore, there is more room in which the ball can fall. The other is that although the ball has a greater target to hit, chances are that on a chip shot the ball will be traveling at a greater rate of speed. If the ball is traveling quickly, it might be to your advantage to have something there to deflect it into the hole, such as a flagstick.

If you have been playing golf for any amount of time, you have seen this last theory work both for and against golfers. I have seen people hit the flagstick when the deflected ball popped right into the hole. On the other hand, I have also seen a beautiful chip that had a little too much speed hit the stick and get deflected to the right or the left. I suggest that if you ever have a downhill putt or chip in a situation where there is the possibility that the ball will increase in speed quickly, leave the pin in the hole. However, if you have an uphill putt or chip, by all means take the flagstick out. Again this is all your own taste; just try not to place too much importance in your mind on whether the flagstick is in or out of the hole. Make your decision and then focus more on the line and speed of your putt or chip.

Pitching

The most common question on the short game is, What is the difference between a chip and a pitch? Well, there is not really that much difference. Pitching is simply swinging the club farther on the backswing and, in doing so, cocking the wrists. The result of a pitch shot is a lofted trajectory, and the clubs used for such a shot are the pitching and sand wedges. Traditionally, the chip has been described as when the wrists do not cock and, of course, the pitch as when they do. This is not completely true because on some chip shots you will use your wrists, and with some pitches you will use very little wrist.

I think your intentions are what determine the difference between these two shots. If you have a very short shot (maybe 2–6 feet) and your desire is not necessarily to loft the ball, that is a chip. If you have a longer shot, in which you need to loft the ball, that is a pitch. A pitch shot will usually require a half to three-quarter backswing.

This shot is somewhere between a full swing and a chip in technique. Like the chip shot, what will determine the distance the ball will travel will be how much of a backswing you take. Your forward swing should be equal to or greater than the distance of the backswing. Your setup should be the same as with the full swing, except

SPECIAL POINTER FOR WOMEN: *After cocking the wrists on a pitch shot, it is not uncommon to see an uncocking of the wrists as the first move back toward the ball. Remember, do not intentionally uncock the wrists. Always feel that the hands are moving with the club head. Never let the wrists throw the club head at the ball. That will result in a shot that is a major real estate purchase or one that would be better suited to bowling!*

the feet should be slightly closer together, and your stance should be open—the same as with a chip shot. You will have an open stance because you want to see both the hole and the ball at the same time. Remember, we are not looking for power with this shot; we only want accuracy. This pitch shot is just a miniature version of the full swing, so the same principles of the full swing will apply. Because the pitch requires more of a back and forward swing than the chip shot, the wrists will cock.

The idea of cocking the wrists seems to confuse people, and a frequently asked question is, "When do the wrists cock on the backswing?" The wrists should cock gradually. When you set up to the ball, your hands have a certain spatial relationship to the club head, meaning the hands are slightly over or ahead of the ball. On the backswing they should keep that relationship. The only way they can do so is to start hinging about hip high, but for your purposes, think of the club head as always slightly leading the hands on the backswing, and you will have accomplished your goal of cocking the wrists.

There are several different types of pitch shots you can use, depending on the type of shot you are planning to hit. Let's say you need a lofted shot that will carry over a sand trap to land on the green. You might want to use your sand wedge because it has more loft than a pitching wedge. With either club, you are going to open your stance and your club face. You will play the ball left of center, with your weight leaning slightly toward your right foot. When playing the ball more to the left, make sure your hands are positioned over or slightly ahead of the ball. Never allow the hands to get behind (to the right of the ball). Since the club face is open, you will need a little more of a backswing than usual, because you will lose distance in the ball's trajectory.

Assume your regular swing posture and make a three-quarter swing. On your follow-through, be sure that you keep yourself bent over. Do not try to lift the ball in the air by pulling your body up. One reason for an

Hands behind the ball at address.

open stance is to allow you to see the ball and the hole at the same time. Another is that this stance will create a very steep backswing path that will force a descending blow to the ball. Any time you have a descending arc, the ball is going to pop into the air. When making a lofted shot it will be important to address the ball with this slightly open stance.

Let's say you have a pitch shot that is level with the green. You only need enough loft to keep the ball from rolling off the green. Position the ball toward your right foot. You can have your feet slightly open, but keep your shoulders square to your target line and place about 60 percent of your weight on your left side. Take back the club with a three-quarter swing. Upon swinging through your shot, you do not have to use the same amount of follow-through as you did on the backswing. Rather, you will swing through about half the amount in which you swung back. This should ensure that the hands lead firmly through the ball, resulting in a lower trajectory. This shot also comes in handy on very windy days. Experiment with different pitch shots, employing the principles that I have discussed, such as ball and weight position as well as open or square stance. Remember, your creativity is a key factor in developing a good short game.

> *Myth:* **Women are excellent short game players.**
>
> *Reality:* **Because of male-biased teaching methods, women who have received a great deal of such instruction are usually worse at the short game than men.**

One reason many women have a problem with their short game is not from lack of talent, but rather from male-biased teaching methods that have put them at a disadvantage. One method taught to women is the pendulum chip shot. As we have seen, this is not a good swing thought. It will take the feel out of the chip and force the larger muscles to work, making it far too mechanical for such a sensitive shot. This is particularly destructive to women because of their bustline. When you lock your arms into a pendulum type of position, you are also forcing them in by your chest. This promotes far too much body motion when you swing the club and will usually make you top the ball. So the next time you hear someone say, "Pretend your arms are like a pendulum," don't listen. Swing the club with your hands and the smaller muscles of the body, not stiff-armed and with the larger muscles.

The Ladylike Short Game

What I call the ladylike short game is when a woman feels she has to hit the perfect lob shot and have the ball roll gently into the hole. *This is not necessary!* We often forget that the idea of pitching is to get the ball into the hole. It doesn't have to look good. What we are looking for are results. If you want to use your driver and roll the ball to the hole, go ahead and do it. All we are concerned about is getting the ball to drop into the hole, not how it got there. As important as finesse is to the short game, it should go hand in hand with creativity. If you want to hit the ball with the club upside down, go ahead and try it, and if it works, use it. Except for a few fundamentals, cast dogma aside and don't care about how it looks.

Putting

The Grip

For the full swing, placing the club in your fingers was important. With the putting stroke, the opposite will be true. The club should be positioned in the palms of the hands. Putting the club in the palms restricts your wrist movement, and this restriction will be important for a consistent stroke. Often this wrist action results when the right hand tries to hit at the ball. In the putting stroke you want the left hand to lead firmly through the stroke, and putting the club in your palms helps you achieve this. Once you realize that you want to grip the club in your palms, the grip you use will be your choice. You want one that will reduce your wrist motion yet also provide you with the touch or feel that is so essential for putting well. If you use the overlapping grip on your full swing, you might want to keep that grip and just slide the hands under the club so the shaft is more in your palms.

Grip the putter in the palms of the hands to restrict wrist motion.

You can also try a reverse overlap grip. Instead of having the little finger of the right hand overlap the index finger of the left hand, you will do the opposite: The index finger of the left hand will lie on top of the little finger of the right hand. This grip gives the left hand a little more dominance, which should make it easier not to use the wrists.

Another popular grip is to assume your normal grip (only locate the club more in the palms of the hands). Then take the index finger of the left hand and lay it across the fingers of the right hand, pointing straight toward the ground. This also helps to firm up the left hand, giving it greater ability to lead through the stroke without using the wrists. Again, this is your choice. Experiment with different grips until you find one that you feel comfortable with.

A very important part of the grip is pressure. You should grip the club so you can feel the weight of the putter head in your hands. Do not grip it too loosely because this will leave the putter head out of control. If you grip the putter too tightly, this will usually force the putter head outside the target line on the backstroke. It will also force you to use the larger muscles of your body. Time and patience are needed to establish proper grip pressure, but it is well worth your while in the long run!

The Stance

When you address your putt, make sure that the ball is positioned left of center. It should be almost off your left heel, the same position you would use with the driver. The reason for this position is that you want to catch the ball on the upswing. When this is done, the ball will roll with a top spin, which will enable it to stay true to its path. You might want to position your feet so that they are pointing left of the target in an open stance. You can also stand with your feet parallel to the target line, as you would with a full swing. Some golfers like this position because having parallel lines makes alignment easier. You can also close your feet to the target by pointing them right of the target. This position is rarely used, but if it helps you see the putting line better, by all means use it! Try to make sure at your address that your hands are aligned straight over the ball or slightly in front of it (more toward the target). This will enable the left hand to lead through the shot and keep the wrists out.

Whenever you set up for your putt, remember to bend from your knees, hips, and arms. Every time you bend, you segment your body. This segmentation is important because it disconnects the body into independently working units. For example, when you bend from your hips, your upper body can move fairly independently of the lower body. When you bend your arms at the elbows, the hands and forearms can do the swinging, as opposed to having the shoulders direct the swing. Since we want minimal body movement when putting, this segmentation is important. When you bend from your hips, you disconnect the upper body from the lower body, allowing your legs to maintain a firm base. When you hunch your shoulders slightly, you make them move a little more freely, rather than forcing them to move precisely with the upper body. Bending at your elbows ensures the shoulders will not dictate the stroke but will allow your forearms to work freely. This freedom in the forearms is essential to obtain the touch or feel that you need to make putts. By touch or feel, I mean something that is sensed rather than contrived. So whenever you set up for a putt, my first recommendation is to bend from wherever you can. This does not mean crouch, but bend enough to segment your body. After you have segmented your body, place your head slightly behind the ball. This will enable you to see both the ball and the cup at the same time.

One thing to remember about body positioning: You want it to be the same every time. Ritual is a very important part of putting. In a tense situation you should keep the same method, pace, and positioning as in your practice sessions. I always watch the way people pace themselves on the green when playing a tournament. This can be a good indicator of whether their game is beginning to fall apart, particularly in match play. They begin playing at a normal pace, using the same ritual on every green; then after a bad hole they increase the speed of their setup and start to hurry or sometimes even get very slow. Either way, it is no good. They have essentially come out of their game and have changed their ritual.

Alignment

You can have the best putting stroke in the world, but if you do not have the correct alignment, it isn't worth a cent. Problems with visual perception can make this a very difficult task for some golfers. However, the majority of golfers and even the visually impaired can learn proper alignment. You have to start by imagining a straight line. Take a string or a ruler, put masking tape on a carpet, or take any straight line you can find, and practice bringing the putter straight back and through. You will have to realize that the putter can only go straight back for a certain distance before it starts to move to the inside. We want this to happen because the hands should always maintain the same proximity from the body as at the address. While the hands and club head are moving, the shoulders are also turning, keeping the club head on the proper path.

Once you have learned to visualize a straight line, the next step is learning how to approach the ball. The approach for putting is similar to the full swing. You should stand directly behind the ball so that the ball is between you and the hole. Visualize a straight line extending from the ball to the hole (assume that there are no breaks). From here, walk into the shot. To walk into a shot, you approach the ball from the rear with your putter in your left hand, always looking at the ball and the hole. Slowly move to your left, and place the putter's head so it is behind the ball and facing the hole, never taking your eye off the imaginary line. Now that you have the club face pointed toward the hole, adjust your body so it is in the address position that I have recommended. From this point, take the club straight back and through. If your alignment is correct, the ball will drop. Having the putter's head in line with the hole should always be your first concern; then get your body situated. Professional golfers in tournaments almost seem to stalk the putt, staring intently at their line until they are set up to make their stroke. Never approach a putt from the left side. This will almost always leave you aiming to the right. Also, never approach the ball from the rear and place your putter blade on the ground facing the hole and then move your body to the left. This will also usually open the putter blade, leaving it pointing toward the right.

The Stroke

There are a few basics to stick to, but overall, the stroke should be all your own style. One basic is that the back-stroke determines how far the ball will roll, and your follow-through should be equal to the amount of your backstroke. For example, if I want the ball to roll a short distance, I will take the club back a short distance and follow through that same distance. Too many golfers attempt to control the distance the putt will travel by decelerating on the follow-through. Many golfers find it very natural to come to a dead stop when their putter comes in contact the ball. This makes them feel as though they are in control, but in reality they are not!

The stroke should be straight back and through, with both hands moving with the club head. When the hands move with the club head on the backstroke, the shoulders will turn. The turn will be with the shoulder caps, not with the left side of your upper torso. This turn will put the club head on a path that will eventually move inside your target line on the backstroke. So although we want the club to go straight back and through, the farther your backstroke the more the club head will move toward the inside. If you attempt to take the putter straight back more than 20 inches without permitting the club head to move toward the inside, it will force your shoulders to dip downward. Be careful of this because it will create a motion that is an under (your backstroke) and up (your forward stroke), which will not consistently strike the ball in the same place. So be sure on your backstroke you do not feel your shoulders being pulled down. Remember that your shoulder caps will remain level on the backstroke. They will turn slightly to allow the club head to move toward the inside after about 20 inches on the backstroke. This might sound familiar because it is the same principle that applies to the backswing.

The shoulders are turning on the putting stroke, but you do not want them to dominate the backstroke. It is the arms and hands that will sense the putt. A swing thought that seems to help some golfers is to let the back of the left hand lead through the stroke. This will ensure that the club head is moving with the hands and minimize wrist movement.

> *Myth:* The putting stroke should be a
> pendulum motion.
> *Reality:* Do not think of a pendulum when
> you are making a putt.

When I discussed chipping, I referred to this same myth. The putting and chipping strokes are very similar in that both require the use of the smaller muscles of the body to get a "feel" for the shot. When someone thinks of a pendulum motion, usually they picture a stiff, rigid motion directed by the shoulders. The shoulders do turn when you putt, but you should not use them as the foundation for the stroke. You want to feel the weight of the putter's head in your hands and let your shoulder caps initiate the backstroke while setting the path for the putter. The pendulum swing is harmful for chipping, but it is disastrous for putting. The putt requires more touch than the chip shot, and there is less margin for error. So when you set up to your next putt, erase the thought of a pendulum motion. Let the shoulders initiate the backstroke, allow the hands and club head to swing to the right, and return through to the left.

Although some good putters have used their wrists in the putting stroke, I suggest keeping your wrists still. Make sure your hands keep the same relationship to the club head as at your address.

Tempo

The rhythm of the putting stroke should be very smooth. Although the putter is accelerating on the follow-through, the tempo on the forward stroke should feel the same as the tempo on the backstroke. You might want to say slowly to yourself, "B a c k and t h r o u g h," and use this as your tempo. Do not try to increase your speed on your forward stroke. Your putter's speed will increase naturally if you let it. I strongly suggest establishing a forward press with your putting stroke (see Chapter 3 on the forward press). Creating a consistent stroke from a completely still beginning is almost impossible. With the full swing you were permitted to press forward with different parts of your body; on the putting stroke you will press forward with your hands only. Remember, the forward press is used to trigger the backswing, and when putting we want our hands to move first. It is important for the hands to press forward.

When forward pressing, do not alter the club face's alignment to the hole by opening or closing the face. You simply want a slight press to enable you to rebound. Some golfers prefer to press into position by having the hands slightly behind the ball at address, and then pressing the hands forward into position. Whichever way you prefer is fine if your press does not alter the direction the club face is pointing. To establish a smooth tempo you might try not grounding the club at the address. When you set up to make your putt, place the club head on the ground directly behind the ball and then lift it slightly so it is not touching the grass. Now make your stroke. You should feel a smoother take-away and follow-through. This also helps to keep the club head from accidentally stubbing the ground on the backstroke.

> *Myth:* **Take the putter back slowly.**
> *Reality:* **If you take the putter back too slowly, chances are it will be on the incorrect path.**

In regard to backswing speed, the same principles of the full swing apply to the putting stroke. You never want the club head moving too slowly because you will lose your rhythm and momentum. In the putting stroke, you want a gentle stroke but "gentle" does not necessarily mean slow. Once you get yourself set in your address position, press forward and gently let the hands swing back and through, in an even tempo. When you try to swing too slowly, you will end up either stubbing the putter head or taking the club on the wrong path. Where you should be extra careful is on short putts. A short putt can produce a lot of tension, and it is particularly important for you to swing the putter in an even tempo. If you take the putter back too slowly, without any type of momentum, chances are you will jab at the ball rather than stroke it. And I can guarantee that *you* will be sunk—not the putt!

Visualization

Concentration and visualization go hand in hand in the putting stroke. First, you want to visualize the exact line the ball is going to roll on, and see it drop into the hole. Next, you want to concentrate. By this I mean block out all conscious thoughts and just keep that picture in your mind. As soon as you step onto the green the visualization process should begin. For example, notice all undulations as you are walking around the green, trying to get a feel for the break. Imagine your putt dropping into the hole from all different angles. The best place to position yourself is directly across from the ball, on the other side of the hole. Try to get a mental image of your putt rolling toward and then dropping into the hole. Every time you crouch to see the undulations, imagine a ball and how it would roll into the hole. The most important part of this process is not only focusing on the line but actually seeing the ball drop into the hole. You want to see the putt through to its completion. So many golfers visualize the correct line leading to the hole, but very few try to imagine the ball actually dropping into the hole. You should rehearse this so well mentally that the actual putt will just follow the path of your imaginary one.

Rehearse this several times while you are standing directly behind the ball. Then as you walk into your putt, keep visualizing that line—do not lose it! If for any reason your concentration is broken, simply step back and start all over again. It is best to practice this type of visualization on the practice green. There you can do all your visualization without having to worry about holding up the foursome behind you. When you get a routine, try to make your every movement on the green have a purpose. That way you will move as quickly and efficiently as possible. Routine is a very important part of putting, and you want to make sure that whatever ritual you establish on the practice green you bring to the golf course.

Whenever I watch Jack Nicklaus putt, his concentration amazes me. I can almost see his mind directing the ball onto the correct path, willing the ball into the hole. In putting it's important to scramble the conscious process and let the subconscious take control. Putting is very much a mental part of the game, but good physical basics work with this mental process to make a good putting stroke.

Selecting the Right Putter

When selecting a putter, you are looking for a club that is properly weighted and balanced. If you are a beginner, you probably cannot tell the difference from one putter to another. If you are an experienced golfer, you can probably tell what feels comfortable and permits a smooth putting stroke. Beginners selecting a good putter should stick to the top of the line by any reputable manufacturer. These clubs usually have the weight distribution and balance to make them good quality putters.

If you are still uncertain which putter to get, buy it from a local golf course professional. She or he can tell you which putter has a better "feel" and would be suitable for you. Whenever a student of mine questions whether one of her putters is any good, I have her bring it to a lesson . . . where I can try it out. I can tell when I pick up a putter and make a few strokes whether the club is good or not. This comes from years of putting. Once you acquire a feel for putting, you can tell if the putter helps you transfer that feel into the putt. If the weight distribution is off on a putter, you will have a difficult time getting a feel for the proper stroke. Buying the club from a reputable golf professional is probably your best bet.

I have known golfers who have owned a closet full of putters, their theory being that when their stroke goes bad they will just switch putters. Hearing this, you would probably think that this was all in their heads, which could well be true. However, maybe some physical factors in their strokes validate their need to switch putters.

Sometimes your grip pressure, stroke, or setup changes, making the putter that you used to think was the greatest no longer work correctly. There are two ways to correct this situation. One is to switch to another putter and accept whatever it is that has changed your stroke. The other is to work to find out what exactly has changed and try to restore your old stroke. I found one putter that worked well and have stuck to it since. If I start to have problems or lose my confidence, I just practice that much more to get my stroke back to normal.

There are times when you are playing different golf courses that have dramatically different speeds for which you might want to change putters. The speed of the green refers to how far and quickly a ball rolls on level ground when a moderate stroke is applied. If you play a course with fast greens, you might want a light putter so you can gently tap the ball. You might also want one with a delicate shaft so you can feel the weight of the club head better; this will give you a better touch. So you might want to have a couple of different putters handy when you play courses that you know will have unusually fast or slow greens.

I have addressed the possibility of physical reasons for suddenly finding your putter unusable; now I would like to address the mental reasons. I don't think anything in golf is as demoralizing as when you are hitting the ball well but can't sink a putt to save your life. As soon as this happens, everything feels uncomfortable, particularly your putter. The putter you once thought was so great is now obsolete and standing in the way of your shooting a decent round. This is when you, like many golfers, may walk into your club's pro shop and ask the pro to recommend another putter. After finding a new putter, you convince yourself that this will be the saving grace of your game. Basically, you are on a psychological high. Confidence is a tremendous factor in golf, and if buying a new putter can make you feel confident, then go ahead and do it! However, realize this confidence will probably be short-lived. It won't be too long before you are cursing your new putter, and you may decide to buy another or even go back to your old one. This becomes a psychological game, and you will end up with a closet full of putters. After you have gathered about five different putters, this is usually the time you decide to give your original putter one more try, and if it works you will wonder why you ever left it! You will probably promise yourself to never again stray from your original putter. After all, this was a good old friend who saw you through many good rounds of golf as well as many bad ones. However, your faithfulness will probably be short-lived; your putter will wind up back in its familiar corner in the close; and you will start your search once more for the perfect putter.

Myth: Women are great putters!

Reality: Neither men nor women reign
supreme when it comes to putting.

Putting requires intense concentration, nerves of steel, and an almost innate touch. I guarantee you, man or woman, if you have the correct line and distance, that ball is going to drop. For any woman who does not hit a long ball, this is the true equalizer of the game. If you can one-putt regularly, you can play golf. There is nothing more demoralizing in a golf game than when you know your opponent cannot hit the ball as far, as straight, or as accurately as you, but when she gets up to the green, watch out— she sinks that putt every time. Use this to your advantage! Remember, it does not matter how you made that birdie. All that is important is the number on the scorecard.

9

Reading
the Green

*The length, grain, and type of grass, as
well as a green's undulations and speed,
determine how a ball will roll.
Calculating these variables is called
reading the green. Good putters not only
possess a good stroke but also excel in
their ability to read greens.*

Once you have mastered the putting stroke, the next important part is learning to read the green. You can have the best stroke in golf, but if you can't get the ball rolling in the right direction, it is not going to do you any good. Reading a green relies heavily on your visual perception. If you have a problem with depth perception or judging distance, you might be in trouble. The way the green breaks depends on many different factors, such as the green's undulations, the type of grass, and any peculiarities specific to the course that you are playing (local knowledge).

The main part of reading a green is to supply your subconscious with all the information possible about the putt. To get this information, view the putt from different perspectives. The behind-the-ball perspective gives you a feel for the line and curvature of the green. Simply stand two feet behind the ball in a straight line with the ball and the cup, and get a bird's-eye view of the putt. Now crouch down and try to get a perspective that is almost at ground level. I find the closer I get to the ground the easier it is to see the slope of the green. When you view the putt from behind the ball, you are getting a feel for the line on which the ball is going to roll. To get a perspective of depth or distance, you will want a side view. Stand to the right or left of the ball about halfway between the ball and the cup, and take a look at the distance you are going to putt. Now move to the opposite side of the cup, looking toward the cup and the ball. This ritual should give your subconscious enough information to make your putt.

The only problem with this routine is that it takes time. Try to get information about your putt as quickly as possible. Although the putt may be important to you, remember that you have three other people waiting to make their putt. As soon as you walk up to the green to repair your ball mark, you should be looking for any breaks or undulations on the green. You might want to think of your mind as a computer. You are supplying it with as much information as possible so it can make its best judgment. Since everyone has different visual perceptions, you might want to try a different routine that is more suitable for you. That is fine; just remember, get as much information as fast as you can. Caddies can be a great help, and many pros would be lost without their advice around the green. I have seen pros who had nice putting strokes but couldn't read the greens match up with good caddies and suddenly they're sinking putts right and left!

When you are having putting problems, try to figure out why you missed the putt. Were you hitting the ball too hard? Were you simply misreading the greens despite a good stroke? Was the ball breaking in one direction consistently? This makes it much easier to correct your problem.

You have probably heard someone ask, "Why didn't my ball break like yours?" You have to realize the putting stroke adheres to the same principles as the full swing when producing spin on the ball. Sometimes when you think the putt is straight, the ball will drift slightly to the right or left. It is not the green that has caused that to happen, but rather your putting stroke. As in the full swing, when you cut across the ball (right to left, depending upon the direction the club face is pointing) it will produce a spin. If you cut across a putt and the club face is square, this will make the ball turn to the right and appear to break in that direction. Make that same motion with the club face pointing to the left and you will pull the ball. An old hustler's trick is to produce such a spin, making the ball appear to break to the right. So his opponent makes his putt expecting the ball to break right and when it doesn't, he naturally misses the putt. So be sure that it is the green forcing the ball in a direction, not your putting stroke.

If you have the chance, always practice on a fast green. The faster the green, the truer the putt. I learned to play golf and putt on slow Bermuda greens, and during those years my putting stroke was not the best part of my game. As soon as I started putting on faster greens, my stroke improved tremendously. With a fast green, it is much easier to develop a sense of touch. On a slow green you develop a hitting rather than a stroking motion. Some golfers like to use different putters to match the greens they are playing on: a heavy putter for slow greens and a light putter for faster greens. I personally find this to be too confusing. I have used the same putter for the last fifteen years. When I putt the different greens, I do not adjust for it physically (by changing putters); instead, I make mental adjustments for how I am going to hit the ball. For example, if I have an uphill putt on a slow green, I do not think of stroking the ball, but rather of hitting it squarely and firmly to about three-quarters of the distance to the cup. If I were making the same putt on a fast green, I would take aim directly toward the hole and gently stroke the ball. It is all according to the golfer's own preference, and it takes time to develop such feel. On a slow downhill putt, I hit the ball firmly one-quarter of the distance and let it roll the other three-quarters. With a super-fast green, I might hit the ball off the toe of the club. The reason for this is to keep the ball from springing from the sweet spot. (The sweet spot is the area on the putter than when struck, produces the best response.) If you feel it is easier to just change putters and use the same stroke, go ahead and do it. The old adage in golf, "If it works, use it," definitely applies to putting.

10

The Sand Game

The sand game is very different from any other part of the swing. One reason is that when you hit the ball from the sand you cannot ground your club. Grounding the club is golf jargon for letting the club rest on the sand (or ground) at address. Only on your downswing can the club touch the sand. Also the idea is not to make contact with the ball but to hit the sand behind the ball and let the force of the sand make the ball go into the air. These are just two examples of the difference between the sand and regular swing. In this chapter I will give you a complete description of the proper execution required for the sand game, from setup to swing.

Set up to the ball as you would for a normal swing, but instead of having the club face square toward your target, you should have it open (see illustration). By opening the club you should lay the club head so it is more lofted. The problem is that when you do this, the club will point toward the right. You will have to adjust for this by moving your body to the left until your club face points directly toward the target. Your body should be at a forty-five degree angle to the target line (see illustration on page 106). The club

Open club face.

Open stance.

should be elevated about one half-to one inch off the ground and should be positioned about an inch behind the ball. The ball should be positioned so it is almost in the middle of your stance. Place your weight slightly to your left side; this will create a descending blow on the ball, enabling you to hit the sand first. Your posture should be the same as with the full swing: Bend from the hips and let your arms hang. When hitting out of the sand trap, be especially careful that once you have established your posture you maintain it throughout the swing. A slight upward motion with the torso can cause you to either top the ball or hit it "fat." (Hitting the ball "fat" is when you hit the ground before you hit the ball.) Be very careful not to get too much lower body movement in your backswing. You simply want to turn the shoulders and cock your wrists. Lower body movement in shifting sand can be disastrous. When you swing the club through, you should employ the same upper body motion that you did in the full swing as the arms and hands swing through. This will pull your weight over toward your left foot and your upper body will release, leaving you looking at your target on your finish.

> *Myth:* **Keep looking at the sand even after you have hit the ball.**
>
> *Reality:* **As in the full swing, your upper body will release on the follow-through, so at your finish you will be looking toward your target.**

Keeping the head completely still in the sand trap can lead to much trouble. As I have discussed before, you always want acceleration in the downswing. When you keep your head still, you are preventing this acceleration from happening. This is especially bad in the sand because you have a very slim margin for error. When you hit the ball fat off of grass you can still get some distance, but when you make that same swing in the sand, that ball is going nowhere! I know it's hard, but you really have to concentrate on following through on your sand shots and not on keeping your head perfectly still.

Your backswing and follow-through should be similar to your full swing, only you are going to take a half swing. The shoulders are going to turn; the wrists are going to cock; and on the follow-through you are simply going to let the arms and hands swing back through the ball in the same manner that they swung away from the ball.

Do not try to force the club head at the ball. This will result in either hitting the ball too thin or hitting the ball fat. You must think of your arms and hands as swinging with the club head (see illustration).

When you first set up in open stance, it will feel very contorted. You'll feel as though your body is pointed in one direction, the club in another, and the swing path in yet another direction and quite frankly, that is about right! Once you have gotten your body in this position, you will want to dig your feet into the sand by sliding your heels to the left and then to the right. This does three things: It lowers your body in relation to the ball; it plants your body firmly so there is very little body movement; and, since you cannot touch the sand with either your club or your hand, you must get your feel from your feet. The "feel" that we are looking for determines the consistency of the sand. The softness, hardness, or loaminess of the sand will be important. This part of the swing is similar to putting and the short game in that it is all feel or touch. Certain fundamentals are required, but you want to develop the ability to sense the shot. The first is important because by lowering your body in relation to the ball it will make it easier for the

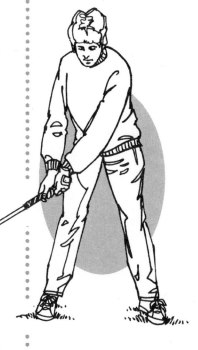

Hands swinging with the club head.

club to move through the sand. And the second is important because in the sand trap you want as little lower body movement as possible. The more you move the more the chance of a shot that is hit incorrectly. Another important part of the sand shot is that you should bend from your hips as you did for the full swing. Again, this will put you in a posture that you should maintain throughout the shot.

Myth: **Try to hit one to two inches behind the ball.**

Reality: **You set up with the club an inch to two inches behind the ball, but never try to force the club head to enter the sand. This will result in a fat or topped shot. A topped shot is when the top half of the ball is hit, resulting in a shot that usually rolls along the ground.**

I think one of the reasons the sand game is so difficult for many golfers is the element of control. Golfers who are so fearful of sculling the ball or hitting it fat become rigid, and they end up trying to control the shot. Whenever you start trying to control the club head, you're in trouble. You must remember at all times to swing the club, not direct it toward the ball. Most people have been told to aim precisely one or two inches behind the ball and deliver the club head to that spot. So intent are they at accomplishing this that they end up either slowing their downswing or just plain throwing the club head at the sand. Either way will result in disaster.

You must always keep in mind that you are executing a motion in golf. Your destination is not the golf ball or hitting two inches behind the ball in the sand, but rather a complete motion where even if blindfolded you would still hit the ball. Yes, you do want to set up to the ball with the club about a half-inch in the air and about an

SPECIAL POINTER FOR WOMEN: *The sand is one area where a woman's natural use of the body to generate power might be a hindrance. Be aware that too much body movement in the sand can lead to a mishit. As I stated before, you want as little lower body movement as possible in the sand. A common error that many of you will probably be able to relate to is the tendency to straighten out your body on the follow-through—almost as if you were trying to lift the ball out of the trap with your body. Remember, keep yourself tilted from the hips on the same spine angle on your follow-through. Do not do this by keeping your head still! Never keep your body in its posture by keeping the head bent over.*

(continued)

inch-and-a-half behind the ball. But do not try to make the club head enter the sand at that exact point. This is a very difficult thing to do in the sand because your margin for error upon hitting out of the trap is so limited. For example, if you are hitting a fairway wood, you could top the ball and still get some distance or hit the ball to the right or left and still not be in too much trouble. However, if you are in a sand trap and top the ball, it may go into another trap, the water, or the rough. Any way you want to look at it, you are probably talking an additional two to three strokes on the hole. When you are in the fairway and hit the ball a little fat, it is still no great loss because the ball will at least get some distance and put you a little closer to your target. However, if you do that in a sand trap, watch out! The ball is going nowhere.

So, you see that there is a lot less margin for error in the sand game. This, in turn, promotes apprehension about the shot, which tenses the muscles, which inhibits your swing, which makes you lose acceleration on the down-swing, which gives you a domino effect resulting in doom!

This will just cause you to lift your head on the follow-through. Feel yourself bend from the hips and stay bent from the hips. One thing that might force you to straighten out your back on the follow-through is trying to make the club hit into the sand, as opposed to letting the hands swing with the club head. The ideal divot for a sand shot is not a deep divot, but rather a shallow slice of sand that is removed when swinging through. Remember, this is an explosion shot. Explosion shot is golf jargon for a shot in which the club never comes in contact with the ball but forces the sand to raise the ball up into the air.

11
Troubleshooting

The Reverse Pivot

As we saw, on the backswing the weight should move naturally over to the right side. When this weight shift does not occur but instead shifts to the left side, it is what we call a reverse pivot. From my experience, the most common reasons for a reverse pivot are:

1. The shoulder turn is incorrect. Usually the golfer is trying to turn her shoulder under her chin and the shoulders end up turning on too steep a plane, making it impossible for the weight to shift.
2. She is trying to keep her head over the golf ball on the backswing. When this happens, the weight cannot shift to the right because the club is being swung back.
3. Her right leg straightens out on the backswing. When the right knee does not remain flexed, it cannot receive the weight shift. This results in a reverse pivot.
4. On the backswing, the wrists are not hinging vertically but are hinging on a more horizontal plane. Remember, the shoulders and hands will travel on two different planes. The shoulders are moving

Reverse pivot.

horizontally while the wrists are cocking vertically. When you get this "round house" type of backswing, the weight will not shift to the right but will move over to the left side as you swing the club back.

Myths That Lead to a Reverse Pivot

- "Keep your head down."
- "Turn your left shoulder under your chin."
- "Pick a spot on the golf ball and focus on it."
- "Feel like you're looking over your left shoulder at the top of your backswing.
- "At the top of your backswing, your left shoulder should point at the ball."

Bending the Left Arm at the Top of Your Backswing

In Chapter 3 on the backswing I address the myth of the straight left arm. Let me quickly review: You do not want to force your left arm perfectly straight, nor do you want it to break. However, it is all right to bow your left arm. When you find that the left arm continually breaks, there is definitely a problem.

1. Make sure you are not gripping the club too tightly. This tension will keep the wrists from hinging correctly and force the arm to break.
2. Do not think of keeping the right elbow tucked in at your side on the backswing. When you do this, your left arm has no choice but to break down.
3. Sometimes the right hand, in an effort to dominate on the backswing, actually pulls

the club in toward your body. When it does so, your left arm has no choice except to bend.

4. If your wrists are weak, bending the left arm is an easy way to get the club into position.

5. If you are a man and your upper body is musclebound, it is very difficult for smaller muscles such as the wrists to work correctly. You will have to concentrate on relaxing the arms and making sure that the wrists do the hinging, not your elbows.

6. You are overswinging. It is possible that, in an effort to get more power, your subconscious is forcing you to overswing. When you reach back for that little extra leverage, your left arm is collapsing. Remember the backswing is for positioning, not for power.

Myths That Lead to Bending the Left Arm at the Top of Your Backswing

- "Keep your right elbow tucked in at your side."
- "Grip the club in the palms of your hands."
- "For extra distance turn your shoulders more."
- "Drag the club head on your backswing."

Straightening Your Right Knee on Your Backswing

At your address, both right and left knees should be flexed. When you reach the top of your backswing, they should remain flexed. However, when your right leg continually straightens, this can be an indicator that another part of your backswing is forcing it to do so. Let me give you some suggestions that will help solve this problem.

1. If your right knee is straightening, then you are more than likely reverse pivoting. See the section in "Troubleshooting" on the reverse pivot.
2. Your shoulders are not making a level turn on the backswing. They are turning under or dipping. Make sure that they turn on a level plane as dictated by your spine angle.
3. If your right leg is straightening, chances are your left knee is moving down. Try to keep both knees as level as possible.
4. When your right knee straightens, this will jog your right hip in an upward movement. Try to make certain that the hips are also turning on a level.

Myths That Lead to the Straightening of the Right Leg

- "Keep your head down."
- "Turn your left shoulder under your chin."
- "Keep your eye on the ball."
- "Swing like you are in a barrel."

Dipping the Head on the Backswing

Many women dip their heads on the backswing. It usually occurs because of a faulty swing thought. A faulty swing thought is when you have the wrong picture of what you want to achieve in your mind. The following faulty ideas can lead to this incorrect movement.

1. You are trying to keep your head down. Whenever you concentrate on keeping your head down this literally ends up happening; your head moves down on the backswing.
2. You are trying to turn your shoulder under your chin. Any time you start to think of turning your shoulder under, chances are this will pull your head down.
3. For women who lack upper body strength, this downward movement makes you feel as though you are generating more power on your backswing. Remember, you have to retrain your way of thinking about the backswing: It is for position, not for power.
4. Trying to force the hands into a higher position at the top of the backswing: If a pro ever tells you to try to get the hands a little higher on the backswing, watch out. It is common for women to actually lower their body in order to put their hands in a higher position.
5. When you are cocking your wrists on your backswing, make sure that the heel of the left hand is not applying so much pressure that it is pulling your upper body and your head down.

Myths That Lead to Head Dipping

- "Try to keep your head down."
- "Turn your left shoulder under your chin."
- "Get those hands high on the backswing."

- "Use your body to swing the club back."
- "Pick a spot on the ball and stare at it."
- "At the top of your swing, your left shoulder should point at the ball."

Swaying off the Ball

Another common problem seen among women is the tendency to sway to the right on the backswing. As we have seen, when swinging the club away, your head should not be perfectly still, but you should remain well centered over the ball. Usually swaying occurs when you try to consciously shift the weight to the right on the backswing. Unfortunately, it is usually because a golf pro has told you to shift your weight. Here are possible causes of your swaying:

1. You are consciously trying to shift your weight to the right. Don't worry about the weight's shifting. If you swing the club back correctly and keep your right knee flexed, there should be no problem.
2. Your shoulders are not turning on the correct plane. This can get a little complex because two different motions are occurring at the same time. Let me try to explain. When someone tells you that you are swaying off the ball, your normal reaction is to try to keep your head still, which results in the shoulders' turning under, which forces the hips to move the same way the shoulders have moved, which forces the hips to slide to the right; and there you have it, a sway!
3. You lift the left heel on the backswing and you get carried away with it and now you are swaying away from the ball.

Swaying off the ball on the backswing.

4. You are just plain trying to hit the ball too hard and you are throwing your body into the backswing. Remember, the backswing is for position, not for power.

Myths That Lead to Swaying

- "Keep your head still."
- "Try to shift your weight to the right."
- "Turn your left shoulder under your chin."
- "Lift your left heel for power."
- "Push the club away from you on the backswing."
- "At the top of your swing your left shoulder should point at the ball."

Spinning Out

A spinout occurs when the hips literally spin to the left on the downswing. Generally this will force the ball to go to the right, or you will end up pulling it dead left. Either way it is definitely not a desirable shot. The spinout usually results from following the advice to put your hips into the shot to generate more power. This is the opposite of what you want to do. Spinning the hips creates a very weak shot.

I have often thought the reason professionals tell women to put their hips into the shot is because when you look at a picture of a woman versus a man swinging a club, you notice a woman's hip movement because *most women have more to move in the hip department than men!* Nevertheless, this is no reason to throw your hips into a shot. The upper body should be trying to catch up to the hips on the downswing. It never does, but the point is: Do not try to force the hips ahead of the upper body on the downswing. Simply let your weight shift over to your left foot to initiate the forward swing.

Hips "spinning out."

Myths That Lead to Spinning Out

- "Throw your hips into the shot."
- "Try to make your belt buckle point toward your target."
- "The first move you should feel on your downswing is the turning of your hips."
- "Think of uncoiling on the downswing."

Lifting the Head on the Downswing

In previous chapters, I have addressed the all-too-familiar statement, 'Keep your head down." I think anyone who has ever touched a golf club has been told to do this. And if you have been out playing golf with your husband or boyfriend, you probably have heard it enough to last a lifetime. The thing that is so terrible about this is the more you try to keep your head still the more it will pop up. If you feel like you just can't keep your head down this means something is forcing your head up. The following are a few reasons the head feels as though it is popping up.

1. When you try to keep your head too still on the backswing, it will force the shoulders to turn on too sharp a vertical plane. The result is that on the downswing the shoulders will be forced to move under and up, forcing your head to lift.
2. On the downswing, instead of allowing your weight to transfer to the left, using the lower body, you are using your upper body to transfer the weight.

3. You are throwing the club head at the ball: Instead of having your arms and hands lead on the downswing, you are letting the club head get ahead of them, which will force you to pull up at impact.

4. You are swinging with a reverse pivot. This reverse weight shift is similar to the first reason. If your weight tilts to the left on your backswing, it will then shift to the right on your downswing, forcing your head to lift.

Myths That Lead to Head Lifting

- "Keep your head down."
- "Turn your left shoulder under your chin."
- "If you swing the club correctly, you should see your makeup on your shoulder."
- "Keep your eye on the ball."
- "Feel like you're swinging in a barrel."
- "Pick a spot on the ball and try to hit it."
- "Watch the club face hit the ball."
- "Finish with your hands high and let it fly."
- "At the top of your swing, your left shoulder should be pointing at the ball."

Shanking the Ball

A shank shot occurs when the hosel, rather than the club face, hits the ball on the downswing, which results in a shot that goes dead right. Shank shots can occur sporadically or can happen with every iron shot you make. Anyone who has ever had a bout with the shanks certainly knows how devastating to the morale they can be. The shank shot seems to be much more common among men than women.

Still, many women seem to suffer from this malady on the green. I think what protects women from the shank on the full swing is their natural tendency to use rhythm and timing to hit the ball, as opposed to men's tendency to use forearm strength. However, if you do suffer from the shanks, these few pointers will help.

Forcing the club face to point down the target line can lead to a shank.

1. You are trying to open the club face on the backswing rather than permitting the club face to open naturally with the turning of the shoulders.
2. You are trying to keep the face of the club pointing down the target line instead of permitting the toe of the club to point toward the sky on the follow-through (see illustration).
3. You are starting your downswing with the spinning of the hips.
4. Your arms are too stiff, particularly on the chip shot.

Myths That Lead to Shanking

- "Rotate your forearms on the backswing."
- "Keep the club face square to your target line, swinging forward."
- "Feel your right shoulder turn under on your downswing."
- "Keep the back of your left hand pointing toward your target on your follow-through."

Overswinging

A common problem seen with women's backswings is the tendency to swing the club back too far. If, at the top of your backswing, you can see the club head dangling, with your peripheral vision, then you can be quite certain you have swung the club back too far. These few tips might help solve this problem.

1. When the shoulders start to turn, the wrists should begin to cock. Do not let them cock at the top of the backswing because this will lead to a loss of control.
2. Turn your shoulders ninety degrees; do not go any farther than this.
3. When you swing the club back, the arms and hands should be traveling faster than the turning shoulders. Do not move everything at the same speed as this will lead to an overswing.
4. If you are reversing your weight shift on the backswing, you will definitely see the club out of the corner of your eye.

Myths That Lead to Overswinging

- "Really turn those shoulders to get more power."
- "Take the club back in one piece."
- "Let your wrists cock naturally."
- "Delay the wrist cock."

Topping and Hitting Behind the Ball

When you top the ball you are hitting the top half of the ball, which gives you a very low trajectory or the ball literally rolls on top of the ground. When you hit behind the ball, you hit the ground before you hit the ball. You would think that these two shots would have completely different causes, but they don't. As a matter of fact, they come from the same source, only with a different result. The usual cause is trying to make the club hit the ball. This creates a casting or throwing motion. Once you have done this, anything can happen, from hitting two inches behind the ball to just rolling it on the ground. A common feeling when you top or hit behind the ball is that you have lifted your body. Just remember, the reason you lifted your body was that your hands had thrown the club head at the ball. Your body and head had no choice at this point other than to lift up. A consistent pattern of hitting behind the ball or topping the ball generally means problems with the general swing motion and will require the help of a good golf professional. However, I will give you tips that might help.

1. On the downswing, simply allow the arms to swing through the ball on the same arc that they swung away from the ball.
2. Do not try to force the club head to hit the ball.
3. Make sure at address you are tilted from the hips and try to maintain this spine angle through the swing.
4. Make sure the wrists are cocked and firm at the top of your backswing. Being out of control at the top (club head pointing toward the ground) can make you hit behind or top the ball.
5. Make sure you are not reverse pivoting (leaning on your left side at the top of your swing).

Myths That Lead to Topping and Hitting Behind the Ball

- "Pick a spot on the ball and try to hit it."
- "Really put your hips into it on the downswing."
- "Turn those shoulders to get more power."

- "Try to snap your hands through the release."
- "Try to accelerate on the downswing."

Skying the Ball on a Tee Shot

When teeing the ball for the driver, a rule of thumb is to tee the ball so that the club covers the bottom half of the ball. If you chronically sky the ball (pop it in the air), teeing it lower will not help you. As a matter of fact, it will reinforce the habits that are making you sky the ball. Whenever the ball is skyed it indicates that you have delivered a descending blow to the ball. With the driver you want an ascending blow, to catch the ball on the upswing. When you tee the ball lower, all this does is make you want to hit even more downward on the ball. The funny thing about a descending blow is you will hit your irons nicely, only when it comes to the woods you will pop the ball straight into the air.

With your irons, play the ball slightly left of center. In order to obtain an ascending blow with the woods, position the ball directly off the left heel. You should be able to manipulate the way the club hits the ball by moving the ball's position in relation to the body. However, when you have a swing that delivers a descending blow, changing the ball position will not help, and you will get a swing that works with the irons but not with the woods. The following is a list of possibilities that can cause such a descending blow.

1. You are reverse pivoting (see Chapter 11 on troubleshooting).
2. You are throwing the club head at the ball instead of letting the arms lead on the downswing.
3. Your upper body is lunging at the ball on the downswing.

4. The club is out of position at the top of your backswing (usually laid off, pointing to the left).

5. Your shoulders are turning downward, not level, on the backswing.

6. Your hips are spinning out on the downswing.

Myths That Lead to Skying the Ball

- "Keep your head down."
- "Turn your shoulder under your chin."
- "Try to see makeup on your shirtsleeve."
- "Get those hips into the shot."
- "Pick a spot on the ball and try to hit it."
- "Turn your right shoulder under your chin on the backswing."
- "Turn your belt buckle toward the target on the downswing."

Hitting the Ball to the Left

Although there are many reasons why a ball will go to the left, checking the position of the club face at the top of the backswing is the first place to start in solving the problem. Ideally, when you swing the club back, the club face will be in an open position, pointing toward the right. From this position the club will square up to the ball during the downswing and then point toward the left on the follow-through. (At the top of the backswing if the club face points toward the sky, we call this a closed club face.) On your downswing, when the club meets the ball, the club face will be pointing toward the left, hence making the ball go to the left. This is actually a very curable problem because you or a companion can see if the club is in the correct position. Other swing faults are not as easy to recognize. Here are a few movements that lead to closed club face:

1. Your wrists are hinging incorrectly. Instead of hinging so the club points vertically toward the sky, the wrists are hinging off to the right.
2. Your arms are initiating the backswing. Remember that the shoulder turn is the first move you should make on your backswing.
3. You are trying to make the club face point toward the ball as you swing the club back.
4. The hands and wrists are moving on a more horizontal plane instead of letting the wrists cock vertically.

Myths That Lead to a Closed Club Face

-   "Swing the club to the inside on your back-swing."
-   "The back of the left wrist should be flat at the top of your swing."
-   "Really turn those shoulders for power."
-   "At the top of your backswing, your right hand should be positioned as if you were holding a tray."

Collapsing the Left Elbow on the Downswing

On your downswing, when you feel your left arm collapse (bend at the elbow), you can be pretty certain you have thrown the club head. Your wrists have used the shaft of the club to try to direct the club head at the ball. When this occurs, the right wrist will supinate and the left elbow will bend (see illustration). Also when this occurs, the left elbow will stick out on the finish, resembling something like a chicken wing!

Left elbow collapsing and right wrist pronating on the downswing.

Myths That Lead the Left Elbow to Collapse

- "Watch the club face make contact with the ball."
- "Throw your hips into the swing."
- "Women should grip the club in the palms of their hands."
- "The hips and legs are solely responsible for power in the golf swing."
- "Think of uncoiling on your downswing."

Stubbing Your Putter on the Backstroke

When you stub your putter, the club head actually hits the ground on the backstroke. This is usually an intermittent problem that happens when you are under pressure. Let me give you a few causes that will help prevent this from happening again.

1. You are gripping the putter too tightly. This can cause the hands to try to push toward the ground.
2. You are swinging the putter too much with your shoulders. When your shoulders move, you should be able to feel the weight of the putter's head in your hands.
3. Your hands have somehow gotten behind the putter head on the backstroke. At address make sure your hands are ahead of the putter head, to the left over the ball. And keep this same position on your backstroke.
4. At address you are putting too much pressure on the putter head in a downward direction (grounding the club). Before you begin your backstroke, slightly elevate the

putter head so it is no longer touching the green, and begin your backstroke from this position.

Myths That Lead to Stubbing the Putter

- "Make a pendulum-type stroke with the putter."
- "Swing the putter with your shoulders."
- "Take the putter back very slowly."
- "Rest the putter head on the ground directly behind the ball before your backstroke."

Picking Up Your Club on Your Backswing

If you are always being told that you pick up the club on your backswing, let me explain what is happening. The shoulders must initiate the backswing. As they are turning, the wrists can cock. But it is essential that the shoulders are turning while the wrists cock. If at any point in your backswing, your wrists hinge without having the shoulders turn, that is when we say you have picked up the club. This usually happens at the beginning of the swing. The wrists snatch the club away before the shoulders have had a chance to turn. It can also happen later in the take-away if the shoulders stop before they have reached their ninety-degree turn. This is a little less common, so we will address the former, that is, the wrists' initiating the backswing. Here are a few tips that might help you with this problem:

Hands picking up the club on the backswing.

1. Usually golfers who pick up the club do not realize that they are doing this. You first want to be able to feel the difference

Hands lead backswing.

between a correct swing (in which the shoulders lead) and an incorrect swing (in which the wrists lead). The best way to do this is by using a mirror. First make a swing intentionally starting with the wrists; then make a swing purposefully starting with the shoulders. Try to practice this at least fifteen minutes a day.

2. After rehearsing in front of the mirror, when you hit balls on your take-away try to feel your left arm in straight alignment with the shaft of the club and keep it as such until about hip high.

3. Another exercise is to try to make your hands go back first, not your club head (see illustration).

4. Try putting more tension in your left arm. With your arm in a tense position, it will be much more difficult for the wrists to dominate.

5. As I have stated in my discussion of the unnatural nature of the swing, it is not uncommon when performing an athletic feat to have a natural inclination to use the stronger parts of your body. It could be that you have very strong hands, and they are trying to dominate the backswing by snatching the club. In this case, try to relax your grip pressure and focus on your shoulders. If possible, do any type of exercise that will increase your forearm and upper body strength. This could prove to be a major benefit.

6. Make several swings, trying not to cock your wrists. And when you are making a full swing, forget completely about the wrists and focus on your shoulder turn.

Myths That Lead to Picking Up the Club

- "Keep your head still."
- "Keep your eye on the ball."

Whiffing the Ball

There is hardly a shot more dreaded in golf than the whiffed shot (completely missing the ball). It happens quite frequently to beginners but even average players experience a whiff now and then. Beginners whiff most often when they are under pressure. The pressure will most likely come from hitting the ball in front of other golfers. Average players may experience an occasional whiff when they are in trouble, such as the rough or in the woods. The common element between both the beginner and the average player is that they are trying to direct the club head to the ball. And as we have learned, anytime you do so you are in trouble. You might try an experiment in which on one swing you simply let your arms swing back and through, hitting the ball. Then intentionally try to make the club head hit the ball (do this in a practice area where there is not a hard surface, to avoid injury to your wrists). When swinging through, feel your wrists throw the clubhead. I don't care how good a golfer you are, if you intentionally throw the clubhead at the ball with your wrists, you will never hit it. I often do this when I demonstrate to large groups how not to swing a club. With my best intentions I am trying to hit the ball, but I am throwing the club head and there is just no way I can hit it; the club is just too out of control.

Here are some things you might want to do if you have just whiffed the ball and are afraid it will happen again, or if you feel a whiff coming on:

1. Loosen your grip. The more pressure you put in your grip, the more control and

steering your swing will have and the greater the probability for a whiff.

2. If you have just whiffed the ball, do not try to swing again as quickly as possible, pretending no one has noticed. First, relax the pressure in your grip. When you swing the club and then immediately attempt to hit again without releasing your grip, the pressure will increase ten-fold.

3. Take some practice swings, using the swinging arms drill (see practice drills in Chapter 13).

4. Do not stare at the ball when you go on to make your next swing. Rather, envision a path that the club is going to swing on so the ball is just in the way.

5. After whiffing a ball, immediately relax your shoulder muscles.

6. Do not focus on the ball, but think of swinging in a tempo, such as "one-two-and-three."

Myths That Lead to Whiffing a Ball

- "Keep your head still."
- "Keep your eye on the ball."
- "Keep looking at the ground even after you have hit the ball."
- "Hit down and under the ball."
- "Watch the club head make contact with the ball."

Flying Right Elbow

A flying right elbow is when the right elbow points toward the side or to the sky at the top of your backswing. Usually this is a function of the right arm's trying to dominate on the backswing, but there can be other causes, and I have listed a few here.

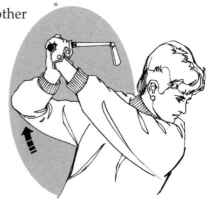

Flying right elbow.

1. The right arm is dominating. Check your grip pressure and make sure you are not squeezing tightly with your right hand. Also check your hand position on the club at address, and make sure you are not gripping the club in the right palm but rather in the fingers. If you are using the baseball grip, change to either the overlapping or the interlocking grip. We want to do anything possible to loosen the right hand's control on the club.

2. At address, make sure that both arms are hanging straight without tension and that the right elbow is not locked straight. The arms should be symmetrical, with the right and left arms relaxed at the crease (where the forearm meets the upper arm). A good way to make sure your arms are relaxed is to get a friend to lightly pat your forearms right at the crease several times, or until you feel your elbow bend slightly .

3. Make sure when you start out that your hands are positioned slightly ahead of the golf ball. This position should leave the back of your right wrist slightly cupped.

4. At the top of your backswing, picture your right arm forming the letter L.

5. Try to get your wrists to cock earlier on the backswing. When the wrists cock, this should encourage the right arm to fold. Also make sure they are cocking. A lot of times you think your wrists have cocked but what has really happened is that the right elbow

has hinged and your wrists are remaining relatively straight.

6. At the top of your swing, feel as though you could wave to someone with your right hand.

7. If you do not have one, establish a forward press, and make sure that before your take-away you pump your arms at least four times.

8. Make sure you are not reverse pivoting (see the discussion of the reverse pivot under "Troubleshooting"). When you reverse pivot, at the top of your swing your weight will be predominantly on your left side. When this happens, it is not unusual for the right elbow to fly out. So make sure that your weight is on your right foot at the top of your swing.

Myths That Lead to the Flying Right Elbow

- "Turn your shoulder under your chin."
- "Keep your eye on the ball."
- "Keep your head down."
- "Delay the wrists from cocking on your backswing."

12

Trouble Shots

In comparing golf to tennis, a friend of mine once commented, "Tennis players would appreciate golf a lot more if they had to play their bad shots." And this is true. In tennis if you make a bad serve, it is considered out and you get another try, which would be a mulligan in golf. (Every time you hit the ball in golf, it should be recorded as a stroke. When a golfer does not record a stroke, and this action is approved by the other members of the foursome, the non-recorded stroke is called a mulligan.) In other words, you could hit the ball into the other court on your serve or hit it a half-inch out of bounds, and you would be penalized equally. One of the difficult things about golf is that when you make a mistake you pay for it. The severity of the mistake will be proportional to the amount of punishment unless, of course, you can make a comeback. And that is where your trouble shots become so important. The ability to recover from a bad shot is as important as making a good shot. Here are a few tips that might help when faced with trouble.

Whenever you are in trouble, your first intention should be to get out of trouble. Do not try to make the comeback shot of the year. You have to develop a level head to assess the trouble you have gotten yourself into and decide how to get out while incurring the least damage possible.

Hitting the Ball from the Rough

When you are in deep rough, you will want to take a lofted club and aim toward the fairway. The deeper the rough the more club head you will want. So for example, if you are in very deep rough, simply aim toward the fairway and use your pitching wedge. In moderate rough, use an eight iron and, of course, in milder rough you can use the same club that you would use on the fairway. The main idea is to be honest about what you think you can do with the shot. Getting the ball out into the fairway should be enough in extreme conditions. The last thing you want to do is to hit the ball back into the rough. Losing a stroke in golf is not terrible. There is always the possibility of chipping in or making some fantastic comeback putt, particularly if it is early in a round—let's say on the front nine. Always remember, you have holes to play and in golf anything can happen.

When you execute a shot from the rough, the idea is to make the club head hit the ball as soon as possible. You do not want any interference from the grass, so position the ball off your right foot. It is also advisable to use a faster wrist cock on your backswing. This gives you a descending blow to the ball. Any time a ball is hit with a descending blow it will force it into the air. However, be careful. Once you cock your wrists, do not uncock them immediately on the downswing. If you do this, you will miss the ball. Do not try to make the club head hit the ball (which is the same as intentionally uncocking your wrists on the downswing). This will also lead to a whiffed shot.

Hitting a Ball out of a Divot

As in the rough, you will want to give more of a descending blow to the ball so position it a little right of center, more toward your right foot. However, beware:

because of this position, the ball will probably move toward your right, so aim slightly toward the left. And when selecting a club, the worse the situation, the more lofted the club should be.

Hitting the Ball from a Buried Lie in the Sand Trap

A ball that is buried in the trap is not a difficult shot to hit if you use the proper technique. Set up in the sand the way you normally would except do not open the club face—rather, close it. You do not want to hit the ball (driving it farther in the sand) but set the club so it will return about a half-inch behind the ball. Close the club face about twenty-five degrees. On your backswing, once your shoulders start to turn, hinge your wrists as quickly as possible. Now let your arms lead while coming down and the ball will pop directly out of the sand. The only problem with this shot is it will not create any backspin so the ball will roll quite a bit once it hits the green. This is really a fun shot to practice, and once you get good at it you will never fear a buried lie because it is one of the easier shots to hit in golf !

The Punch Shot

A punch shot is usually employed when you have something you have to go under, let's say a branch of a tree. The ball is punched, giving it a low but strong trajectory. This can be a tough shot for many women because a good punch shot that carries a decent distance usually requires strong forearm and upper body strength. It's a disadvantage in one respect but it might be an advantage from a different perspective, however. Often stronger players get too much loft on the ball from executing the shot incorrectly and end up getting themselves into trouble.

Women who don't have that strength will not hit the ball as far, but they will also stay out of trouble.

To execute the punch shot simply let the hands swing with the club head. Try to keep your hands in a straight line with the shaft of the club, and keep the club head as low to the ground as possible on your follow-through (see illustration). I advise using a club with the least amount of loft possible and playing the ball more toward your right foot. Ideally, a three iron will do, but if the rough is high or thick you may want to use a club with more loft. A punch shot is similar to a chip, only there is more backswing and consequently more follow-through. If you swing through correctly, you will feel your weight being pulled over to your left foot. Having the weight transfer in this manner ensures a low flying shot. It will feel more like a jabbing motion, hence the name "punch shot." This is a very handy shot to use around the golf course so practice it and try to become as proficient with it as possible.

Punch shot follow through.

Hitting a Ball That Is Lower Than Your Feet

If you live in a hilly part of the country, you know how much trouble having to stand with the ball above or below your feet can create. If you are on a steep grade with the ball positioned below your feet, realize that, through no fault of your own, the ball will probably veer to the right. In this position, the angle at which the club face meets the ball causes this to happen. Simply be prepared by aiming toward the left.

Whenever you are standing on the side of a hill, do whatever it takes to put your body back in balance. If you are standing with the ball lower than your feet do not lean forward, but plant yourself firmly with your weight leaning toward your heels. Position the ball so it is centered between your feet. Put a little extra bend in your knees and use a longer club. If the grade is severe, stay away from your woods. Go ahead and swing the club, but really concentrate on staying in your posture (down and through the ball).

Hitting a Ball Situated above Your Feet

Almost everything is going to be the opposite of when the ball was below your feet. When hit, the ball will most likely go to the left, so compensate for this by aiming right. You will want to use a club with a shorter shaft but you also want distance, so use a less lofted club. Lean slightly forward and swing, trying to stay in your posture as much as possible. If you want to use a longer iron, simply choke up on the club (place your hands down on the shaft, toward the metal) to shorten the length of the shaft.

Hitting a Ball on a Downhill Slope

First, position the ball so that it is located right of center. The more severe the grade the more to the right you will position the ball. You will want to use a lofted club, and again, the more severe the grade the more loft you will want with your club. Place your weight so it is fairly equal, and consider leaning a little toward your left side. Since the ball is being played off the right foot, the shot will have a very low trajectory; that is the reason for choosing a lofted club. You play the ball off your right foot because you want the club head to return to the ball without taking much ground. This is a difficult shot so don't expect to get any distance. Just get yourself pointed in the correct direction and hope for a lot of roll.

Playing the Ball on an Uphill Slope

Position the ball toward the middle or slightly left in your stance. Lean slightly toward your left foot. You will want to take a less lofted club because the ball is likely to take a high trajectory. Go ahead and take a swing but expect to lose distance because of this trajectory.

Hitting a Ball with No Room to Take Your Stance

Let's say your ball is within one foot of a tree. Obviously there is not enough room for you to stand between the ball and the tree. Instead of assuming your normal right-handed stance, you might try addressing the ball left-handed. When you do this the club face will be pointing in the opposite direction so you will be hitting the ball with the back of the club, not the club face. Of course, the ball is not going to get any loft, but at least it will get away from the tree and be closer to the hole.

Flyer Lies

Be careful of flyer lies. A flyer lie is one in which the ball springs unexpectedly off the club face. A flyer lie with a chip shot can cause the ball to go far past the targeted hole. A typical flyer lie is when the ball sits on very fluffy grass. When the club head makes contact with the ball in this position, it will tend to spring off the club face. Of course, this results in a shot that lands far past the intended target. The hardest part of dealing with such a lie is learning to identify it. Usually you realize it too late, after the ball has flown past the hole. It helps to look for the ball's being positioned on grass that is fluffy.

When executing the shot, swing a little more gently than usual. Also, when you set up to the ball, do not ground the club; rather, position it so the club covers the top half of the ball.

Hitting over a Tree

When hitting over a tall object, you should position the ball so it is off your left foot, with your weight leaning to the right. Use as much of a lofted club as possible without sacrificing distance. This is one of the few times in the golf swing that I would encourage you to wait until after you have felt the club head hit the ball before you look to see where it has gone. This shot, as with the chip and the putt, creates a great deal of anticipation. It is not uncommon for golfers to look to see where the ball has gone before they have even hit it. When you do this you will usually top the ball or even hit it fat. Just try to keep yourself in your posture as much as possible through the swing *and do not peek!*

Most golfers get into trouble when trying to go for distance. They sacrifice the necessary loft to get over the tree, and the ball ends up hitting the very tops of the tree. Just try to get over the tree—do not try anything fancy!

Ladies, Be Careful

Since you already have the tendency to use your whole body on the swing, your body may lift in an effort to get the ball into the air. When you execute this shot, you must be very careful that you stay in your posture and let the loft of the club face do the work for you.

13

How to Practice

You see many golfers on the practice tee, but few really know how to practice. Even the golfers who take lessons and are working on specific swing problems are not practicing correctly. Here are a few ideas that will make your practice session more enjoyable and productive.

First, never try to correct too many problems at once. Identify all the problems you and your instructor discussed during your last lesson and start from there. Let's say, on your last lesson you worked with cocking your wrists correctly, the proper way and angle to bend your body at address, keeping your left foot on the ground on your backswing, and letting your follow-through pull your weight toward your left foot. Do not put all these swing thoughts in your head on the practice tee, but rather, *rotate your thoughts*. Hit five balls working with your wrists; then forget about your wrists. Hit five more balls thinking about your left foot; then forget about the foot. When you do this, you will slowly incorporate changes into your swing without painfully obsessing on each one. Also, ration balls for each swing thought. In my example, I listed four swing problems. If you have sixty practice balls, reserve ten for each problem. The remaining twenty should be used to relax and clear your mind. You might want to hit five balls with each swing thought in mind (a total of twenty) and then hit five balls just thinking of your tempo or as much of nothing as possible.

This can actually be fun and a good mental exercise in concentration.

A truly neglected part of a practice session is alignment. First, completely forget about your swing problems. This practice really does not require balls but if you can, hit a few. Take a club and lay it on the ground so that it points slightly right of your target. Next, gripping a club, assume your proper address so that the club face is perpendicular to the club on the ground. Make sure your feet are parallel with the club and that your hands are the correct distance from your body. Then place the club that you are holding on the ground in front of your toes. Both clubs should now be parallel. Grip a third club and put your body back into position, with your toes touching the second club. The club face of your gripped club should point toward your target, and your feet should be parallel to the target line. You are now ready to hit golf balls. Change your targets frequently so you get the feel of aiming in different directions.

I think we have all seen golfers who aim too far right, and if you point this out they will probably say, "No way—I'm pointed right on line." If you place a club on the ground to show them where their feet and club face are pointed, their reaction is one of disbelief. It is very easy and quite natural for one to get misaligned. The reason I say natural is that when your body points to the right it is unconsciously trying to create leverage to hit the ball farther. In some sports or skills this may be helpful, but in golf it will result in a shot that goes either dead left or slices to the right. You have to train your mind not to do this. And the best way is to routinely practice your alignment.

I remember when I started teaching, I would see people make great improvements in their swings but they would always come back with the same complaints: "I hit the ball so well with you standing there, but when I am on my own, nothing works." I always thought they were exaggerating the situation until I went to a local course to play one day and saw several of my students playing.

Their swings did not look even remotely similar to the ones that I had been teaching. After my round, I spoke to the head professional about the situation and he replied, "You range professionals lead a very sheltered life. You do not have to witness what I see every day. You can work with people on their golf swing for a half hour and watch everything that you have worked for be destroyed in a matter of minutes. All that it takes is for them to set one foot on the golf course."

Well, now I agree with him, and I also think that one of the biggest problems is that one foot is pointed in the wrong direction! Once your body is misaligned, there is no way you can execute a normal swing. You are going to unconsciously end up compensating for this lack of direction. Take the example of the woman who points her body to the right on every shot; this will result in her grooving a swing that comes over the top, which will create a pulled or sliced shot. So you can spend a half hour teaching her the correct swing plane and in nine holes of golf see this mastery destroyed. A practice session devoted solely to alignment is really not a lot to ask when you consider the consequences.

I am often asked how many range balls a student should hit in between weekly lessons. I would love to give a magic number that would guarantee improvement, but unfortunately no such number exists. Hitting a golf ball does not improve your swing; it is how you practice and what your intentions and swing thoughts are that will make a difference. The presence of a golf ball is important for conditioning a swing. Someone could make beautiful practice swings for hours on end, but as soon as a ball was put in front of them that swing would change. This happens because the ball elicits your body to use its natural ways of making power, which are incorrect in golf. When you practice making the correct swing while looking at the ball, the sight of the ball should elicit the response of a good swing. Where the ball goes is less important than the fact that you are viewing and hitting the ball. You should hit as many balls as possible, but you should hit them intelligently, not emotionally.

After hitting a bad shot at a driving range, your first inclination is to hit another ball. Do not do this. Keep your focus and concentration on what you are practicing. Most ranges will make it easy for you to hit another ball quickly since this is what makes money. There is usually a tray that you can dump your balls in and then with your club easily scoop them onto the mat without having to bend over. Try keeping your balls in the bucket and place the bucket several feet away from you so you have to reach and bend over every time you want to hit a ball. This should slow down your pace and give you time to think between shots. Never hit a ball out of anger; you will accomplish nothing. Practice sessions are not only for hitting balls but to increase your attention and teach you patience. The mental aspect is at least as important as the actual swing.

Visualization should be a large part of a practice routine. Try to imagine different golf holes on the driving range—particularly the ones that are giving you the most difficulty. You might even want to mentally act out playing a hole by changing clubs after each shot. For example, imagine a par five. First hit with your driver, then fairway wood, and then a 5 iron. And when you target-practice, switch your target frequently. It is important to visually change targets and align your body correctly.

Ritual

An essential part of a good golf game is a preswing ritual. When you practice, you should not only concentrate on your swing motion, but also on what type of routine you perform before the swing. In Chapter 8, in the section on putting, I stressed the importance of keeping the same ritual for every stroke. Well, this also holds true for the full swing. A practice session is a great time to ingrain a ritual for yourself. Whenever practicing, always approach the ball from the rear, as you would on the golf course. Keep a club on the ground, perpendicular to your feet, to assure proper target alignment. Every time you approach your shot you should take the same amount of steps toward your ball and try to move your body at the same speed. Remember, you will carry this same methodology and pace with you to the golf course, so just relax and make sure you go through the same routine every time. At first you may find it difficult to discipline yourself in this manner. However, when you do get a routine going, you will find that your concentration level on the course will increase dramatically.

I first noticed how important ritual was to a good golf game when I caddied for a friend who was trying to qualify for the a major amateur championship. This was a thirty-six-hole tournament, and my friend had a very good round for the first eighteen holes. As we started the second eighteen, I noticed that he was walking a little faster than normal and he was setting up to the ball in a slightly different way than he had been. He scrambled on the first four holes for his pars, and then his pace started to increase dramatically. The next thing I knew, he wasn't completing his backswing. It had become short and quick. Even his speech was much faster than normal. I knew immediately that if he was going to qualify I was going to have to get him back in his old pace. I told him how quickly he was moving and that for the next few holes he had to concentrate on walking slower even if he still was hitting bad shots. He did as I requested and it took him about two holes to get his tempo and ritual back. I watched him carefully and if he did anything that I thought was out of his normal routine I let him know. Fortunately he ended up coming in second place and earned a spot at the national qualifier. Ever since that time, I can usually tell when someone is going to start playing poorly (given that I know their normal pace and preswing rituals); I can almost sense their coming out of their game. That is why I tell golfers the more they practice a pace and tempo for themselves the better it will translate onto the golf course.

Internalizing What You Have Learned

Sometimes when working on your swing, you may think you understand what you are doing, but the reality of the situation may be that you have not yet internalized the correct concepts. With some students I have had to correct the same problems over and over again. These students will usually say, "I understand what you are talking about; however, it is difficult to get my body to do it." This usually means that consciously they have an idea of the mechanics involved, but subconsciously they have not internalized my advice. When a swing concept is finally internalized students get the feeling, "So that's what she was talking about." At this point they understand the concept as well as get an idea of what it should feel like.

Everybody learns or internalizes ideas differently. Someone may say, "I understand, I understand," and then all of the sudden say, "Now I really understand." For some golfers this can happen in weeks some in years. Everyone's learning process is different but when it does happen, it will be a sudden insight that takes you to a different level in your golf swing. This is the manner in which distance comes to a golfer. All of the sudden you will hit the ball farther than ever, and the feel of the swing will be effortless. You may hit a couple of balls like this and then it will your distance will suddenly disappear. It will return again where you hit four or five balls at new lengths and then disappear. This process will continue until you consistently hit all your shots at this new length. This newly obtained sense of distance might have been something you had been working on for years or only a few short months. All you can do when you practice is to try your hardest to conceptualize what your golf professional is trying to get you to accomplish, and employ the practice techniques I have offered in this book, and I think you will internalize different aspects of the swing quickly.

14

Different Swings

Myth: **If you are left-handed, you should learn to play golf right-handed.**

Reality: **If you are left-handed, stay left-handed; do not try to play golf right-handed.**

Golf has been and currently is viewed as a sport for wealthy white males. Well there is another criteria that needs to be added: all right-handed males. As you all know, the out-and-out bias against women is common-place but left-handed golfers are frequently viewed with as much disdain. I have never understood the intense dislike of left-handed golfers. I remember when working in a pro shop if a left-handed person was alone and looking for a game, a twosome or threesome would be asked if they minded playing with a lefty. I have asked individuals who did not like left-handed players to explain their bias, and I have gotten answers such as, "They stand on the wrong side of the ball" and "It's not normal for golf to be played like that," and of course, that "it just plain looks funny." I think that more than being directed at left-handed golfers it is just a mentality in golf that if you do not meet the traditional golf image then you should not be on the golf course. Another way to look at it is, I am a right-handed male golfer and I have a terrible swing and really can't play; therefore, I am going to keep all of you in your place by not letting you beat me on the golf course. I think the coming of great left-handed players such as Phil Mickelson will begin to change attitudes, however, the change is likely to be slow.

If left-handed male golfers are disdained, you can imagine how a left-handed female player is viewed in the golfing community. Many women who feel that bias are afraid to play left-handed, fearing total exile from the golfing community. I can't tell you how many times I have watched a woman's swing and, noticing how uncoordinated her body appeared to be, asked if she was left-handed. Her reply was usually, "Yes, but my club pro (or husband, or the person who sold her the clubs) says that I should play right-handed." When I suggest that they start swinging left-handed most lefties are extremely reluctant about changing. Usually I hear excuses like, "I don't want to have to get a new set of clubs" or "My husband wants me to play right-handed." The excuse of not having clubs is somewhat reasonable, as left-handed women's clubs are hard to come by and a new set of clubs can be quite an investment. However, what is the point of paying for lessons when you don't have the correct set of clubs? And the husband who tells his wife to play right-handed fears that people will not want to play in couples events with them because his wife is left-handed.

Asking a left-handed player to play right-handed makes about as much sense as asking all right-handed players to play left-handed. The old theory was that left-handed people have a strong, dominant left arm, which is desirable in a golf swing. The only problem with this theory is that lefties' whole sense of coordination is left-handed and having them swing right-handed should be disastrous. I sometimes swing the club left-handed to get the idea of what it must feel like to be uncoordinated and trying to learn golf. And even though I can swing the club with some degree of success, I could not possibly achieve the level of success that I have swinging right-handed, and I think that most lefties will find this to be true with their swings.

You will find that most golf courses are designed with right-handed golfers in mind, and since 95 percent of all golfers slice the ball, most courses will penalize you for such a shot. But for the lefty, a slice means having the ball curve to the left, so playing left-handed can be a big benefit on some courses.

If you are a left-handed golfer who has been playing right-handed, think about switching back to your natural side. It will take some work getting used to playing this way, but it might make a big improvement in your game. If you have a left-handed child, please do not teach him or her to play right-handed. I have friends who despise golf because they were lefties but forced to play right-handed in childhood. If you are left-handed and want to begin playing golf, do not let any salesperson tell you that you should have a set of right-handed clubs. Insist on purchasing left-handed clubs. When you take lessons, tell the golf professional that you are left-handed and ask if they will have any problem teaching you. A qualified professional who is right-handed should have had plenty of experience teaching lefties, so that should be no problem. And when you get good at golf, turn to your right-handed friends and suggest that maybe if they played left-handed their game would improve. After all, they are standing on the wrong side of the ball!

Two Negatives Can Equal a Positive

We all want to have the perfect swing. But you have to realize that in golf such a thing does not exist. What is a perfect swing for one person may not be for another. We all come in different shapes and sizes, with different physical strengths as well as different mental imagery. What is important is how consistently one plays well. If you regularly go out and shoot a sub-par round of golf, you have an excellent swing. I don't care if the swing is odd to watch; it hits the ball well, and that is all we care about. You could have the most seemingly graceful swing in the world and not have it be effective. This is where most women have been victims: They have been taught to throw certain bodily parts into the swing to make it look pretty, not to hit the ball correctly.

When I lived in Miami, every year I would attend the Doral Open. I would get up early in the morning so I could watch all the professionals preparing for their round on the driving range. I would watch such seemingly perfect swings made by golfers I had never heard of. Their swings looked great on the practice tee, but when they got out in a tournament situation their performance would fall apart. This is what competitive golf is all about. It is creating a golf swing that will survive the most intense pressure. It is not the best looking, but the most effective swing that wins. You can have a different combination of factors that work together to produce a good swing. You can have two bad movements that create an effective move when combined. I often see golfers employ several bad moves in their swings that actually make their swings work.

For example, let's take a woman who forces the club incorrectly to the outside on her backswing. Just because she has done this incorrectly does not mean she will be unable to get back to the ball and make a good shot. Quite the opposite: If she combines this bad backswing with another move that puts her on plane, she might get back to the ball and actually hit it quite well. If she throws her hips into her downswing, it is possible that these two combinations working together will create a well-hit ball. Someone watching her swing might say that her swing is unorthodox but that she hits the ball very well. The reason they might call it unorthodox is because she has combined two moves that by themselves are normally destructive to a golf swing and used them so they are constructive. The reason I bring this up is that I have heard students describe women they play golf with by saying, "That Frances has the strangest-looking swing but boy, can she hit a ball!" The reason Frances hits the ball so well is that she has probably employed three or four faulty moves that produce a positive result. Do not try to mimic Frances. She has an unusual swing that works for her but most likely will not work for you! Also, swings like Frances's are usually grooved in—that is, conditioned through much repetition—after playing for many years. The manner in which someone like Frances develops such a swing is just having one bad move compensate for another bad move, and grooving it in over a period of time.

Let's take our example of the first woman again. She swung the club back so it was outside her line on the backswing and then threw her hips so her hands actually dropped into perfect position. She then did nothing more than just swing through with her arms and hit the ball, and when she did she hit a perfect shot. You have to realize that what makes a swing a good one is the position your body is in at the time of impact. You have probably heard that at impact all great golfers are in the same position. This is true, but the manner in which they get there can vary dramatically. The more superfluous movement, the more your body will rely on timing rather than on mechanics to hit a ball. With a more mechanically correct (little superfluous movement) swing, the mechanics will create proper timing.

Take our friend who on the backswing takes the club to the outside. In order to compensate for this, she throws her hips into the swing, but what if she throws her hips too quickly or if the club was not quite as outside as it normally was on the backswing? Obviously, these deviations could create a problem getting back to the ball. And with a swing like this it will take many years of play and practice to create such a timing. So you see, when swinging the club, you want to create a swing that has as little superfluous motion as possible. With the smallest amount of moveable parts, theoretically you have less room for error. However, some people require this superfluous motion because of their build or their innate sense of timing to hit a nice ball.

The Whiplike and Regular Swing

There appear to be two types of swings that many women employ when hitting the ball. The first uses a whipping action and the second uses the techniques that we have discussed so far in this book. I will call the former a whiplike swing and the latter a regular swing. In the whiplike swing, the golfer uses her upper body to set up a motion that creates a whipping effect. This leaves the club head to emulate the tail of a whip. With this swing, as the body is swinging through, the wrists will release the club head (throwing the club head). While this happens, the body will slightly raise itself out of its position, possibly onto its toes, and the ball will be struck with a good deal of club head speed.

This swing is commonly employed by smaller women and can be quite effective. The only problem is that there will not be much room for improvement. They will hit the ball far but that is the maximum distance they will get. As they get older, they may find that their distance decreases dramatically. Usually golfers who have this type of swing say either they hit their woods better than their irons or vice versa. Also, when they are playing poorly, the ball will have the tendency to tail off to the right. However, when they are playing well, they will play a good game and if their short game is good they may well produce some low scores!

Although this swing can be effective and is employed by many women, I would suggest that if you have this type of swing, change it. And if you are a beginner at golf, try to stay away from it. The regular swing is the one that will be effective for the majority of you, and that is the swing that we have been discussing in this book. But I want you to realize that the golf swing does not have to look perfect to be effective. Remember the woman I described in the section "Two Negatives Equal a Positive," who employed two normally destructive swing moves to create a positive result? Golfers who employ the whiplike swing have exaggerated finishes. You will hear comments like, "That Anne has such a high finish, isn't it great?" or "Martha really gets her body into that swing and boy, does it go." These exaggerated features are a part of literally being out of control of one's finish. For example, consider our friend Anne with the high finish. This finish is probably the result of her upper body's starting the whipping motion, then her arms, and by the time the club head (the tail of the whip)is involved, it is carrying such momentum that it flings up and around, forcing the club's shaft to strap across her back. And in the case of Martha, the same will hold true. She probably sets her upper body in motion, which pulls the rest of her body through, giving the appearance that she has really put her body into the shot. Again, this is not necessarily wrong—it is just part of the whiplike swing.

15

Psychological Troubleshooting

The Yips in Putting

For those of you who do not know what the yips are, I am not sure I want to tell you. A yip, like a shank, can be one of the most demoralizing problems in golf. A yip is when you take the putter away from the ball but cannot seem to come back through to hit the ball. The only way you can get the club to go forward and stroke the ball is to make a sharp, jabbing motion, hence the name *the yips*. Sounds crazy right? That's what I thought until I had a bout with a very bad case of the yips. My bout lasted about six months; and it was making me crazy. I could take the putter away from the ball, but for the life of me I could not bring it back through to hit the ball. The first thing you'll hear about the yips is that they are incurable and that once you contract this mysterious plague, it is the end of your golfing career. Well, from my experience this couldn't be anything farther from the truth. I consulted a friend who was a psychiatrist because I felt the yips might be the golf version of a nervous break-down, and was told the psychological reasons probably rested in a phobic reaction of some sort. I went to a medical doctor, and he told me I seemed to be in good health and he could see no physical reason for this malady. Finally one day when I was on the practice putting green, I got some advice from a retired doctor with whom I frequently played golf. When I told him of all my efforts to figure out what was making me yip, he just laughed and explained to me that a yip starts out as a physical error in your stroke that eventually becomes psychological. He had been observing my putting stroke for the past month (while he was winning my money) and had noticed that on my take-away I moved my body slightly to the right. When this happened the only thing left for me to do was to slide my body over to left, leaving me with a jerky punch at the ball, which was my yip. When I could not correct the problem, it then snowballed and became psychological, destroying my confidence and upsetting my nervous system. But as you see, my malady was firmly rooted in a physical error that I was making. And by the way, I have watched many people since then who yip on short putts, and I commonly see the cause as being the same one that plagued me: too much body motion on the putt.

Shanking the Ball

Another golf disorder that is often referred to as being completely psychological is the shank. I have addressed this issue in "Troubleshooting" and given some myths that lead to a shank. But this is such a common problem I feel that it warrants more attention. First, let me remind you that a shanked shot is a shot that has been hit on the hosel of the club and shoots directly to the right. People who occasionally shank the ball are much easier to cure than the habitual shanker. An occasional shank on the full swing usually occurs when the hands turn clockwise on the backswing. The only real difficulty in curing this is the fact that it is intermittent, and the chances are that the golfer cannot feel the difference between the correct and the incorrect move. However, this case is still quite treatable.

Now to the habitual shanker. I don't think anything in golf feels quite as out of control as the shank. It is a terrible feeling when, no matter what you do, everything from a 3 iron to a pitching wedge goes dead right. It is such a total loss of control that sheer panic is a common reaction. Most of the time it is exactly this panic that causes the next shank. In a normal swing the club moves from the toe's pointing to the sky on the backswing to the toe's pointing toward the sky on the follow-through. With a shank the club face is open, with the hosel hitting the ball first. A common pattern for many people who shank is that their hands freeze at impact, putting the club into a position to shank the ball. The more you shank the more you will develop the tendency for the hands to freeze at impact until eventually the causes of shank become psychological, and you will be afraid to swing the club through the shot.

And what is worse is the reception you will receive on the golf course. No one will want to play with somebody who shanks the ball. And golf professionals particularly—the ones who are working on their own games—will not want to teach you. I have seen a golf pro wear sunglasses during a lesson with a chronic shanker so that the student won't be able to see that the pro is not really looking at his swing. The pro, of course, is fearful that she, too, will catch this dreaded swing disease. So the shanker is actually being treated as a golfing leper. This again has a psychological snowballing effect.

Most problems such as the yips and shanks begin as mechanical errors and turn into psychological errors when no solution is found. The golf swing is twofold; it is a mechanical motion, but it relies heavily on the subconscious. If you have a chronic problem, such as the yips and shanks, do not let yourself become a basket case. Your problem is firmly routed in mechanics, and with good instruction and hard work it can be cured. There are exceptions where the nervous system is shot and someone can no longer hold the putter steady enough to make a putt. Or sometimes there is a psychological problem, with a fear of humiliation or success or failure or whatever. But it has been my experience that 99 percent of the time it is simply a matter of faulty mechanics. So always look to your swing fundamentals to solve any problems. Do not just say, "It must be psychological; I can't get over it."

First Tee Jitters

Usually at the first tee, there is a line of people waiting to tee off. So you might get to the first tee and have five foursomes lined up waiting to start, with nothing better to do than to watch you hit the ball. Many times golfers dread this situation and are so conscious of being watched that they botch their shot. This anxiety is called the first tee jitters. I honestly think every golfer has had those jitters at one point in time. Those who have a case of the jitters will usually score poorly on the first couple of holes, and once they settle down they will start to play well.

I started golf very late in life, so I never had any amateur tournament experience. The first tournament I ever played in was at the LPGA qualifying school. The atmosphere was so tense I was even nervous on my practice rounds. Since I had never played in a tournament, I had no idea what type of score I would shoot. And I became almost phobic, dreading going to the first tee for fear I might dribble (hit the top half of the ball) or worse yet, actually miss the ball! Of course, all this fear was irrational. I probably have whiffed a ball once in my life and very rarely have I topped the ball, but still the fear was there. When the tournament started, I wanted to back out; however, I mustered all my courage and arrived at the first tee, praying for rain. When my turn came to tee off, they announced my name and someone held up a "Quiet" sign. I was so nervous I couldn't think. And I believe it was precisely this inability to think that helped me hit a nice drive right down the center. I bogeyed (one over par on each hole) the first couple of holes but after that I started playing a good game. I actually started looking forward to the tees where there was a gallery. It was then that I realized that I was a ham—I loved the attention! I finished the day on the leader board five strokes off the lead.

Later that evening I spoke to a woman who was a veteran player and told her of my fear of the first tee. She told me that she used to have a terrible fear of topping the ball off the tee in front of a gallery. One day it happened. She hit the ball, and it rolled maybe 20 yards in front of her. After this incident she realized nobody really cared; no one was laughing; and it really did not matter. She now realized her worst fear was really pretty insignificant. This experience enabled her to get rid of those first tee jitters and get on with thinking of where she wanted the ball to go, not where she feared it would go.

As long as you do not slow down play or get in the way on the golf course, there is never any reason for you to concern yourself with what others may think of your golf game. You have paid your greens fees and you have as much right to be there as anyone on the course. And the fact that you are reading this book to improve your game tells me that, although you may think you're not, you are probably better than 95 percent of the golfers out there!

16

Faulty Swing Thoughts

The myths that I have been speaking of generate faulty swing thoughts. Everyone has a concept or a picture of how to execute a good golf swing and tries to think about those ideas when swinging a club. These mental images are shaped from what one sees and reads about golf and also what one feels when swinging a club. Much misinformation is spread by popular golf magazines. How many times have you seen a magazine cover touting a new way to get power, only to see, six months later, that same idea being touted as a way to lose power? I used to read these publications and concluded that every six months the publishers reverse their ideas about the golf swing. So if you read a January issue that tells you to use your hips for power, you can be almost certain that July's issue will tell you that power does not come from the hips. You must remember when it comes to advice on the golf swing, these people are in business to sell magazines. They want you to feel that when you subscribe to the magazine you are going to improve your game. How many of you have eagerly run off to the golf course, attempting to implement the latest golf tip you had read?

Sometimes these magazines give good advice, but most of the time they are telling you to do something that reinforces some myth. For example, a quote on the cover will recommend turning the shoulders for more power. Golfers who read this will go to their local range or golf course and try to implement this into their swing. When they twist their shoulders around, they will get the sensation that they are creating power, so they will immediately think, "Hey, this article's great. It is really going to help me increase my distance." They may even hit a shot that goes farther than any they have hit before. But I can guarantee you that if they keep this up, it will end up ruining their swing.

There are no quick fixes in golf. When you have problems with your swing, generally it is a problem with your general motion, and a magazine article is not going to correct it. What avid female golfer could walk by a magazine stand where a cover story claims to be able to add 15 more yards to her swing, without stopping and at least looking at it!

The Mental Image Doesn't Always Match the Real Performance

I feel that many good players do not know what makes their swings so good. This may have been truer in the past because many new players are pretty well schooled in modern swing thought. But many professionals who play well are the individuals who have helped purport the myths I have spoken of for both men and women.

Many good golfers start playing golf in their youth. When you tell a six-year-old girl to not to move her head while swinging the golf club, chances are the head is going to move even though the child thinks she is keeping still. This is the beginning of a misleading swing thought. As the child gets older, if she is asked what she thinks of on her backswing, she may reply, "Keeping my head still." In reality, the head is not still, but the child has become used to having little movement and describes it as still.

Junior golfers are often told to keep their eye on the ball. Most junior golfers will keep their eye on the ball but their body and head will move properly. If you told adults to do the same thing, they would end up freezing over the golf ball, allowing little or no head or body movement, which, of course, is what we do not want. So you see, starting out, this junior golfer (say, it's a boy) has two ideas in his head that are faulty, and he is not executing them to the precise letter. If he did, he would not have a very good swing. As he matures—let's say he's in his teens—and you ask him what his swing thoughts are, he might say, "Keeping my head down." But what he thinks of as keeping his head down might be the farthest thing from what is really happening. At this point, keeping his head down might mean for him keeping himself centered over the ball or feeling the point where his shoulders complete their turn, but he conceptualizes all this in the phrase, "I keep my head down."

If this same junior golfer were to teach someone his age or older to play golf, he would use the same catchall phrases that he learned as a child. However, telling adults to keep their eye on the ball will make them freeze. As you may well know, adults have a tendency to be much more controlling than children.

You have to realize that golf-playing professionals and teaching professionals are two different breeds. Just because a person plays a good game of golf, it does not mean they know how to critique your swing. The last thing a playing professional wants to do is to give me some advice on what an amateur is doing wrong. Trust me, they are not looking at your swing trying to analyze it; as a matter of fact, they would much prefer not to see your swing at all.

Good athletes are good mimics. They can watch an athletic motion and instantly repeat what they have seen. Unfortunately, they are also very permeable. If they see an incorrect motion enough times, they will start to incorporate it into their own swings. When you ask these professionals what is wrong with your swing, most do not know and do not want to know. Their business is making their own swing work. Every golf professional has a professional from whom they receive advice on their swing. Unless they are planning a career in teaching, they're not interested in analyzing an amateur's golf swing. On the other hand, teaching professionals, after viewing so many bad swings, usually have a tough time keeping their own swing in some sort of playing condition. If you watch someone cast the club enough times, you will see that same motion appear in your own swing.

Very few golf professionals can teach a full schedule of students and at the same time go out and play and win tournaments. I had a friend, a club professional, who qualified for five U.S. Opens. Every year, several months before the open qualifying, he would stop teaching and turn his lessons over to an assistant because, as he would say, "How can you look at all those bad swings, and expect to play golf?"

Another way faulty swing thoughts are born is by the myth's perpetuating itself. When someone points out the hip motion and only the hip motion, and you concentrate on this motion you will think the hips are the whole swing! If someone pointed out leg motion and you observed people's leg motion, you might think this was the basis for the swing. If you are told, "Watch how still he keeps his head," to your naked eye plus your belief that it is still, the head will look frozen. When that same swing is put onto video and you can watch it in slow motion, you will notice that the head really does move. So you can see, these myths can be self-perpetuating.

A Picture May Be Worth a Thousand Words, but Not in Golf!

Many golfers and golf pros get some strange ideas about the golf swing from looking at pictures of famous golfers. The most commonly misinterpreted areas are at impact, finish, and downswing. Golfers look at the classic impact position of great golfers and then go to the practice tee or to the golf course and try to duplicate that positioning. The only problem is that the picture that portrays that position is showing one split second in the swing. When you try to replicate the impact position it will take you four or five seconds to do so. And in that time you will be guiding the club, and you will lose acceleration. Golf pros do not physically try to get into such a position; it is simply the result of a good swing. And as I said, they only maintain that position for a split second.

Another commonly imitated picture is the follow-through. Everyone tries to emulate a Freddy Couples follow-through. The picture looks good, but Freddy did not try to make himself finish like that—it was simply a result of his swing motion. If you practice emulating someone else's follow-through I guarantee that will lead to trouble in your swing. People who use video equipment to study the downswing will look to see if the wrist angle is being maintained on the way back to the ball. It is true this is what is desired in the swing. But you do not consciously try to keep the wrists cocked down to the ball. The downswing, if executed correctly, happens so quickly there is no way you can mimic the hand action of a golf professional.

The picture of the hips through the swing is the most misleading for women. Golf professionals will point to a picture of a famous female golfer on the back-swing and say, "See how much she has turned her hips? You should do the same." And then on the follow-through they will again point to the hips and say, "See that hip turn? That's exactly what you want." This could not be farther from the truth. The reason they notice the women's hips more is that *women have more hips to notice!* As I stated in Chapter 3 on the hips' providing a lower center of gravity, you will notice that many good female players have the hips to provide them with this lower center. And this is a desirable physical feature for female golfers. If you looked at pictures of a skinny male with tiny hips, who was swinging the golf club, you probably would not pay attention to his hip movement. But how could you help but notice the motion of a woman's hips in compar-ison? A good male golfer and a good female golfer should have the same hip movement. The only differ-ence is that a woman has more to move.

Another common swing motion often emphasized by professionals is swinging from the inside to the outside on the downswing. Although it may appear from the camera's perspective that the professional is trying to force the club to swing from the inside toward the outside, she is not. Once a golfer has turned her shoulders, the club has been brought toward the inside. If she simply lets the club swing back on this same path, it will return from the inside. As a matter of fact, you should never swing from the inside to the outside. The club comes back from the inside, squares up, then moves back to the inside. This can often be misleading; if you get the wrong camera angle, it will look as if the club is swinging out, not straight down the target line. So you can see, while golf pictures are good to view to get an idea of what you want to accomplish in a swing, do not think that mimicking those positions in a swing is going to help you hit the ball any better.

Reversing Your Thought Process

If there is an area of your game that is not quite up to par that you need to focus on, you might want to try to reverse your swing thoughts. Let's say that your problem area is putting. You might be focusing on the wrong part of the game. It could be that you are too focused on how well you are hitting, or the distance you have hit your drive. Most people tend to put greater importance on where they start (the tee shot) than on other parts of the game, and that level of importance diminishes as they get to the green. To improve your short game you will need to reverse this thought process. When you step on the tee and look toward the green, your thoughts should be simply to get to the green. That is your destination, and it is of the utmost importance. As you approach the green (despite what may have happened to you on the way there), think to yourself, "This is where the game really begins." When you make that chip or putt, think, "This is what the game of golf is all about." Excite yourself; the more meaning and importance you put on your short game, the more your concentration will improve, particularly with putting. When you go to make your putt, give it the same importance and consideration that you do your drive.

My golf school at one time was located at a golf range that had a beautiful indoor facility as well as large putting, sand, and chipping areas. The golf school was separate from the driving range but in all, the facility boasted one hundred tees. On weekends and nice summer evenings the tees would be completely filled. As a matter of fact, people would stand two-deep waiting for an open tee. It would always amaze me that out of all these people, at the most seven would be on the chipping and putting green. As I said, this was no small facility.

There was plenty of room for twenty people to work on their short game.

A stroke is a stroke, whether it comes from an errant drive or a bad putt. The putt may not be as glamorous or fun to look at as a drive is, but it certainly deserves at least as much attention as the full swing. I always tell my students that the full swing is easy. The idea on the full swing is to swing the club back into the same position every time. The hard part of golf is the short game, chipping and putting. You have to determine how much of a backswing to take, and there is so much feel and touch to this part of the game you cannot rely completely on mechanical movements.

Reversing your thoughts can also help in other areas of golf. One is the sand trap. Many golfers dread hitting into a sand trap, and it is this fear of hitting into the sand that actually makes it happen. You may set up to make a shot to a well-bunkered green and think, "Oh, no, please do not let my ball go into the trap! I'll never get out!" It is precisely this logic that will get you into trouble. As soon as you start thinking in this manner your muscles will tighten and you will consciously try to steer the club when hitting the ball. On a good course, sand traps are positioned to frustrate the average golfer. And more than likely, your ball will fall into one of these traps. Instead of fearing the sand, think to yourself, "Gee, if I mishit the ball, I sure would like it to go into the trap. That way I will get more practice at being a better sand player." If your ball does go into the trap, be excited. Think, "This is just as important as my drive, and I am going to really concentrate on this shot." Fear is your worst foe in golf. As soon as you start to fear shots, you have lost the battle. Rather than fearing the shot, get excited about the possibility of executing a shot well and of someday being an excellent sand player.

Another area in which reversing your thoughts might help is when hitting your second shot with water to the left and right of you on a par five. Do not look to

TIP FOR WOMEN: *It is important on the short game that you repeat to yourself that you are just as capable of making a sand shot as anyone else. You may be intimidated by having been outdriven by a man on your tee shot, but when it comes to the short game and sand game there is no reason why you cannot be the best. This does not require distance, but rather finesse. So when you set up to the sand shot think, "This is at least as important as my drive, and I am going to be an excellent sand player someday!"*

your left and right thinking, "Oh no, I am surrounded by water," but rather look to where you want to place the shot and make sure you are aligned properly. The ball may go into the water, but try to keep your thought focused on where you want to hit the ball. If you are slicing the ball, do not compensate for the slice by aiming way right. Stick to your guns and stay focused on the area where you want the ball to land. Compensating for a slice is just going to make you create an even bigger slice. Do this on every hole with every shot: View where the trouble lies and then pick the area where you would like the ball to land. If you are aligned correctly, the ball should go where you have intended. If it does not, this was the fault of your swing, and trying to compensate for it will usually lead to greater trouble.

You might notice that reversing your thought is usually going to change a negative concept into a positive one. But it should be much more than changing "I can't" to "I can." It should be focusing your thoughts as well as not being negative. At the beginning of this section I spoke of changing your focus from driving to putting by saying to yourself when you're on a green, "This is where the game begins." It is exactly this rearranging of thoughts that should accompany a positive attitude.

Play Your Own Game

To play your own game means not to let your opponent intimidate you. Stick to your own game plan and, try to minimize your weaknesses and maximize your strengths. You have probably played golf with someone who outdrives you. This can be very disconcerting, especially if you add pressure to your own swing to hit the ball farther. Once you start competing with your opponent on this basis, you are sunk. If your opponent hits the ball farther than you, accept it; do not try to play his or her game. I have seen golfers play all day, the ball into the rough, never a fairway, and yet score well. For some golfers, this is a normal game plan. Do not watch them hitting the ball from the rough and think to yourself, "This is going to be easy," because it very well might not be. You have to focus on yourself and your own game. Never take your opponent for granted, and never let your opponent intimidate you.

I once knew a man named Buddy who was in his early seventies. When younger, Buddy had been an excellent golfer, and at his present age he was competitive in the club championship. His shortcoming was that he did not hit the ball very far off the tee, and his strong point was that he had a deadly short game. As eliminations went on, I would watch Buddy carefully peruse the tournament board to see who his next competitor might be. The competition was made up of several men slightly younger than Buddy, but the majority were in their late twenties and early thirties.

One day I saw Buddy smiling a sigh of relief over the results of a recent match. I was completely puzzled because a strong young man by the name of Rob had beaten an older man not much younger than Buddy and was to be paired against Buddy in the semifinal rounds. I had thought Buddy would be upset over the results, thinking he would prefer to play the older man. As Buddy was smiling and looking at the boards, I said, "Buddy, what are you so happy about?" He replied, "This is just what I wanted. Give me one of those young kids who hits the ball 280 yards off of the tee any day of the week." He looked me right in the eyes and said, "As soon as they see this seventy-year-old man chipping and sinking every putt, their 280-yard drives are going to go 280 yards straight into the woods!"

And that is exactly what happened. Buddy could only hit the ball 175 yards off the tee, but he was deadly with his short game. He just played the whole round sticking to his game plan. Rob (the young man) thought the older man could not beat him, but as soon as he lost a few holes to Buddy, Rob could not handle it. As Buddy had predicted, those 280-yard drives were going straight into the woods. Rob lost his composure and ended up losing the semifinal round to Buddy, who won two-up with one hole remaining. This is a perfect example of playing your own game. Buddy knew his strengths and weaknesses, and was not intimidated by a younger man who could double the distance of his drives. However, the younger man was overconfident, and though he was on the green in two and Buddy was on in three, Buddy would always sink his putt. As soon as Buddy won a couple of holes, he had forced Rob out of his game. He had Rob thinking, "I'm going to put this old man away. I am going to knock this drive 300 yards." But as Buddy had predicted, it got him into trouble and eventually caused the loss of the match.

So if you are in a match and your opponent is outdoing you in a specific area, do not lose your concentration. Just stay in your shoes and do not come out of your game. Always play your own game. It should be what you know best.

17

The Subconscious Mind

One of the most enlightening parts of playing golf is watching the subconscious mind in action. I was a psychology major in college, and nothing I read or studied in college fascinated me as much as what can and does occur in the golf swing.

The first time I really felt my subconscious take control was when I played in my first LPGA qualifying school. Q-school is the qualifying tournament that enables you to play the LPGA tour that everyone prepares for their entire golfing careers. If you make it through q-school, you get your tour card, which enables you to play the LPGA tour. It was my first professional tournament, and the atmosphere was so thick with tension that you couldn't help but be nervous. I wanted so badly to shoot a good round that my mind felt as though it were paralyzed, and it was exactly this scrambling or paralyzing of my conscious mind that put my subconscious to work. I felt that I was not making the shots independently; something inside of me had taken over and was in complete control. This something was making shots and sinking putts to par holes, no matter what trouble I had gotten myself into. It wasn't until the final four holes that I started to relax, and when I did, my conscious mind took over and I started making a few mistakes. But in all, I finished on the leader board three strokes off the lead.

This feeling is like operating by remote control. Something directs you, and that something is the subconscious mind. Maybe some of you have felt on a chip or pitch shot that the ball would go into the hole, and it did. Well, when your subconscious is really in action, you *know* the ball is going into the hole. It's very strange to know what is going to happen before it actually does.

I have come to view the subconscious mind as that which knows all about your golf swing. For example, let's say you hit your No. 5 iron 120 yards. Now, you are on a golf course and you are faced with a shot that you think is 120 yards, but it is actually 112. Thinking it is 120 yards, you choose your No. 5 iron. When you hit the ball, you end up hitting it fat. You might say you did something wrong in your swing. In fact, it was your subconscious mind that made you decelerate on the shot. When you consciously thought you had 120 yards to go, your subconscious did not accept this and saw the distance to be 112 yards. On your downswing, your subconscious took over and slowed everything down, thinking that if you did hit the ball it would be at least 8 yards past your target.

Now let's say you have a shot that you think is 120 yards when in reality it is 130 yards. Again you reach for your No. 5 iron. Only this time, instead of hitting it fat, you top the ball. On your downswing you feel your body lunging at the ball, trying to muscle the ball, and you do not understand why. It is because your subconscious mind sensed that you did not have enough club to get the ball the distance you wanted, and it tried to help by putting the entire body into the shot.

Water and hills sometimes distort one's perception of distance on a golf course. When you have such an illusory distortion, the conscious and subconscious come into conflict. Assuming that your No. 5 iron goes 120 yards, you are now faced with a hole where there is water between you and the green. The water creates the illusion that the shot is only 100 yards away. Your subconscious knows that it is 120 yards, but your conscious mind tells you it's not. This is where trusting your swing comes into play. Trusting your swing is the same as trusting your subconscious. If you could just close your eyes and swing the club, you would probably land the ball right next to the hole. However, chances are your conscious mind is going to try to intercede, and you will end up trying to force your swing, which will result in a missed shot.

A similar case is if you are on the tee and the hole in which you are playing is a dogleg right, with water on the right side. Your conscious mind, afraid of hitting right, is probably going to try to steer the club head through the ball, trying desperately to make it go straight. When this happens you will decelerate, and of course, this can lead to almost anything, including hitting the ball dead right or slicing. An experienced golfer would look at the hole and not focus in on the negative (the water). They would think about where they wanted to place the ball, not where they feared the ball would go. The difference between the two is that the experienced golfer has learned to trust her swing, which is the same as allowing the subconscious to work. The inexperienced golfer, on the other hand, has let her conscious take over and interfere with her swing.

Although your subconscious knows more than your conscious mind, it still must be trained in certain areas to perform at its best. One example is that on the golf course you will generally tend to set up too far to the right of your target, particularly with your drives. This is done subconsciously, because your subconscious sees a target and, knowing you require distance to get to that target, it will automatically want to align your shoulders and feet right of the target. This will put your body in a position of power so you can swing across your body with some leverage.

This would probably help create power in any other endeavor, but not in golf. Your subconscious has to be retrained to recognize that you are using a golf club and that this positioning does not work, but rather will produce a slice. This topic is addressed further in Chapter 3 in "The Unnatural Nature of the Swing." You will start to realize that the subconscious will naturally help you in many instances and in other instances it has to be retrained to work with the golf swing. Although the subconscious is powerful, I am afraid it is not preprogrammed with the theory of the golf swing! You will find that the better players have trained and learned to trust their subconscious minds. And when you hear players say they trust their swing, they are really saying they have found and learned to use their subconscious minds.

In Chapter 9 on reading greens, I have stated that it is important to feed your mind as much information as possible about a putt. Again, the reason for this is that you are feeding your subconscious mind information so it can make a decision on the putt. When you look at the putt from behind, to the side, and in front of the ball, you give the mind different perspectives that are important to making a successful putt. Even elements such as the wind and the type of grass and its texture are important information for your subconscious. Putting is where you really want your subconscious to come into play. You truly have to envision a path that the ball is going to roll on and not let any other thought get in your way. Concentration is really a state in which you can have a direct route to your subconscious by jamming interception by the conscious mind.

Maybe you have been lucky enough to get the feeling that you cannot do anything wrong. I have described it as being in remote control. But it truly is amazing when you know a putt is going to sink or a chip is going to go into the hole. Again this is all being produced by that incredible internal guru, the subconscious.

Golf Viruses

I have taught students of both sexes who were members of country clubs. It was after several years of teaching these people that I noticed swing faults that seemed to be common to each particular club. At first I thought it was due to faulty instruction at the clubs. But as I investigated, I found this not to be the case. In reality, these people were unconsciously picking up bugs from one another's swings.

For example, one of my male students developed a certain problem in his swing. At the top of his back-swing, his club face was slightly closed. At address his grip looked good, and on his backswing his wrists cocked correctly. I could not figure out what was going on. And then I noticed it: Just before take-away, his right hand very quickly and subtly regripped the club. It would slide slightly under the handle. I have seen people regrip the club on the backswing but never as slightly and subtly as he did. About a week later, out of the blue, a woman from the same club came to me complaining of swing problems. It was an exact duplicate of the man's problem. At first I thought, "What a coincidence." Then during the next two months five people, all from the same club, came to me with the identical problem. If it had been a commonly seen swing error, I would have written it up to chance. But this was such a subtle, distinctive move it couldn't be chance. I later learned that each of these people had played with one another recently prior to the occurrence of their swing problem. I have witnessed similar bugs with members of other homogenous clubs. The golf clubs where the membership is larger and less homogenous seem to have fewer common swing problems.

So for those of you who are members of country clubs, you have a new excuse for not playing well! You can simply explain that your golf swing is under the weather; it must have picked up a virus. I only hope that the cure I give these swings spreads equally as fast.

18

Adults as Beginners

Childhood is the perfect time to learn to play golf. I have found that between the ages of four and eleven children have a very natural golf swing. They have no fear of failure or humiliation and no need for control. Whether the ball rolls on the ground or goes in the air, it's all the same. When children miss the ball, they tend to think it is funny, not embarrassing.

Children are very permeable. You can take an eight-year-old child who has been swinging incorrectly since he was five and change his swing in ten minutes. However, when a child enters the teenage years he tends to become very rigid. If you take a fifteen-year-old child who has been swinging the club incorrectly since he was fourteen, I can assure you that it will take much more than ten minutes to correct his swing.

For men it is more desirable to start learning golf at a young age because their strength then is similar to women's. They do not yet possess the upper body strength that will make them want to slash at the ball. Rather, they will use the whole body through timing and technique (similar to a woman's swing). You will notice that a ten-year-old boy will have a much more natural swing than an eighteen-year-old male.

If you are an adult female taking up golf, you are at an advantage being female, as I have stated, but there are some disadvantages in being an adult. Adult fears of embarrassment and humiliation can be a big stumbling block for the learning process. Many new golfers put too much pressure on themselves, worrying about what others may think. You have to realize that even the best golfers were once beginners. Every golfer has experienced the same frustrations and fears that you will be experiencing. Golf may look easy (as do all sports done well) but it is not. I am always amazed by people who take two or three lessons and cannot understand why the ball will not go where they have aimed. Like anything else you do in life, if you want to be good, you have to work at it. After taking three piano lessons, I would not expect to sit down and play a concerto!

The fear of looking foolish and embarrassing oneself seems to be prevalent in every golfer's mind. If you are a beginner, the best piece of advice I can offer is to get over this fear as soon as possible. You are playing a game and nothing more. Do not let your self-esteem rest on how well you hit a ball, particularly when you go out onto a golf course. You are new at this game, so do not expect miracles to happen, no matter how good an athlete you are.

Missing the ball completely is always at the top of the list of fears for beginners, particularly when they are on the golf course. The worst part of it all is that the more you try to make the club head hit the ball, the more likely you are to miss it. This has been discussed in other chapters, but I will repeat: Never try to direct the club head to the ball. You are simply making a motion in which the ball is in the way. This desire to make the club head hit the ball is a natural tendency, and as you get better in golf you will learn to overcome this instinct. However, in the meantime, if you miss the ball and then miss it again, simply pick up the ball and go on your way. A casual round of golf is not the same as playing in the U.S. Open.

No one is going to mind if you pick up your ball; in fact, you might find that it is greatly appreciated!

Why Did It Go to the Right?

As a beginner, it is normal for you to want your pro to explain why the ball went right, left, or straight. You must remember that at your stage of the game you do not have a golf swing. Yes, you are swinging the club, but the swing is in no way ingrained or repetitive. The chances of your hitting the ball straight are about the same as your hitting it in any direction. Unless you are an expert golfer, usually there are multiple reasons why the ball goes in a certain direction. The first thing you should learn is to swing the club; do not expect or try to make the ball go in any direction.

One reason golf is such a difficult game to learn is that there is no immediate reinforcement for making a good swing. You should realize that you are trying to learn to make the swing that gives you the most consistent results. These results should be the ability to hit the ball in the direction you want, with the distance necessary for any given shot. Unfortunately, in golf, hitting a ball beautifully is possible with a poor swing. Again the reason the swing is poor is that seven times out of ten it will not produce such a result. If you take a beginner or experienced golfer (say, it's a woman) to a driving range and she is hitting the ball very far and straight, naturally she is going to assume that she is doing everything correctly. Well, the truth of the matter might be that she is just getting lucky. She could be making incorrect swings, and still be getting positive results. So you see, the visual reinforcement of a good shot might actually be reinforcing the wrong moves. Someone once said to me, "The trouble with golf is you can't see yourself hit the ball." I then replied, "And even if you could, you wouldn't know what to look for!" This is why you need an experienced individual who knows what makes a swing with a consistent effect.

Unsolicited Advice

Beginning golfers—particularly females—beware! Chances are, like many others, you will become the victim of unsolicited advice. These purveyors of bad golf advice are everywhere and are just waiting to spot a poor neophyte golfer struggling with her swing. Driving ranges are one of the favorite haunts of these people. Between shots they peruse the tee line, hoping to find someone that they feel will listen to their advice.

I find it amazing when I watch golfers who, if they're lucky, break 100 telling each other what is wrong with their swings. Never take advice from these people because they do not know what they are talking about. If they did, they would be golf professionals or could at least break eighty on the course. I guess the psychology behind all this is that they feel inadequate about their own golf game. When they see a beginner who would not know a good golf swing from a bad one, they seize the opportunity to try to impress the beginner with their knowledge and their swing.

Please realize that a truly knowledgeable person would not make any comment about your swing unless you asked them. As a golf professional, if I witnessed a coprofessional with a problem in her swing that I could help her with, I would not do so unless asked. Even if the problem were obvious and I had the perfect solution, it would be completely unprofessional of me to approach her. If she were a good friend, I might say, "Would you mind if I made a suggestion?" If she said yes, I would accept it and get out of the way. Nothing is ruder than to have someone approach you and tell you what they think is wrong with your swing. I cannot tell you how many beginners I have taught who have come back after their first couple of practice sessions, completely confused because someone had offered bad advice. I always ask my students why they pay me for lessons and then go listen to some free advice. Usually the reply is, "I did not want to be rude; he seemed like such a nice man." Telling someone not to bother you while you are working on your swing is not rude. The fault of rudeness lies with the "authority" offering you advice in the first place. If someone approaches you and says, "Do you mind if I help you with your swing," simply say, "Yes, I do." It is your right. Often even better players, after playing golf with someone who happened to play well that day, will listen to that person's advice on the basis that he or she had a good round. Remember that it is possible to play a good game of golf and have a bad swing. A good golf swing is a consistent swing; it lasts for more than just a day.

Etiquette

Etiquette is an important part of golf. The game of golf was designed to be played in foursomes, therefore, it is a social sport. When you play golf you can expect to spend up to five and one-half hours in the close company of three other golfers. The other three could be close acquaintances or complete strangers. Either way, this time should be as pleasant as possible, no matter how poorly you are playing. I will give you a few tips that might help you understand the golf etiquette.

On the Putting Green

The first thing you should do when you approach the green is look for your ball mark (divot) and then repair it. If you see a ball mark that is not your own, repair it anyway. Once you have done this, you should mark your ball. Simply stand in a straight line directly behind your ball and the hole, and place a ball mark behind and as close as possible to the ball. The first person to putt is the one who is farthest from the hole. You will maintain this order the whole time you are on the green. Let's say the woman who is farthest away from the hole putts first, and she accidentally hits the ball too far. If she is still the farthest from the hole, it will be her turn again. If there is any question as to who is farthest away, simply say, "Is it you, or is it me?"

It is the responsibility of the individual closest to the hole to either tend or remove the flagstick. If everyone in your group is close enough so that tending the flagstick is unnecessary, simply remove it and place it gently on the green out of the way. If you think that someone might require the flag to be attended, just ask, "Do you want me to tend that for you?" Usually someone who has a lengthy putt will want the stick to be tended. To do this hold the flag stick so your hand covers the flag and the stick at the same time to prevent the flag from flapping in the wind. Lift the stick slightly out of the cup to make sure it is not stuck. Then stand off to either the right or left to ensure that your shadow is not in the way and that you are not stepping in someone else's line. Once you have done this, remain as still as possible until your opponent or partner has hit the ball. Once the ball has been struck, you want to get out of the way. Again, be sure you do not step in someone else's line.

When a player's ball is situated on the frog hair (the short hair surrounding the green), he does not have the right to have the flag stick tended. He can request that you either take the stick out or leave it in. If he opts to have the stick left in, step to the side out of his line until after he has putted. If he asks you to take it out, remove the stick but do not place it on the ground. Then stand off to the side until after he has putted. When you see that no one else will require to have the stick attended, gently place it on the ground off to the side.

When on the putting green, always make sure you know where all the players' balls are situated, so you do not step between their balls and the hole. This is the surface they are about to putt over and your footprint can cause a missed putt. Watch out for your shadow. There is nothing more disconcerting than having someone's shadow move in front of you as you are preparing to make a putt. Never stand directly in front of or directly behind the target line of someone who is putting. Also, never face someone's back. It is an eerie feeling when you are putting and people are directly behind you. When on the putting green, remember it is not the U.S. Open. You are playing a simple round of golf, so try to read the greens as quickly as possible. It is very frustrating waiting to hit your approach shot while the people in front of you are taking five minutes each to read a putt. If you are the first one to putt out, immediately pick up the flag stick and stand somewhere off to the side. Even though you are probably thinking about your own game, try to show interest and support for the others who are putting. If you are wearing golf shoes with spikes, do not drag your feet when leaving the green. This will tear up the grass. For this exact same reason, some courses have become spike-less, that is, not permitting any shoe spikes to be worn while playing.

In the Sand Trap

Always rake the sand trap after you have hit the ball. Never take a practice swing in the trap (this is a rule, not just etiquette). Never stand in the sand trap while your opponent is getting ready to hit the ball. Wait until she finishes her shot and then enter the trap (again, this is a rule). Do not just rake the area that you disheveled; if you see other footprints and divots, go ahead and rake them also (or as much as you can without delaying the golfers behind you).

On the Course

On the first tee, you will decide the teeing order (who hits first). This can be done as casually as saying, "Go ahead, you're ready," or "Do you mind if I go ahead and hit?" You may also determine who goes first by coin toss or by simply throwing a tee in the air (whomever it points to when it lands goes first). You should keep this order until someone gets a low score, and then it will be their honor to go first.

The one who hits first from the fairway is the one who is farthest from the green. This holds true as long as you are not delaying anyone behind you. Let's say your partner hits the ball into the woods, and she is the farthest away from the hole. If you have people behind you, go to your shot and hit and then help your partner find the ball. If you are the one in the woods and you think you will be looking for a while, you might tell the others in your group to go ahead and hit. Any time you feel that you are delaying someone behind, let them play through. If you are delaying someone with whom you are playing and it is not a match, just pick up your ball. You could say something like, "I got my money's worth out of this hole," pick up your ball, and move onward.

After a shot, always replace your divot (the chunk of grass your club tore from the ground). Be aware of where the other players are and what they are doing. Never stand ahead of a golfer who is about to hit the ball. Not only is this distracting for the golfer hitting the ball, but it is very dangerous for you. I have seen very good golfers shank the ball, and if anyone had been standing to the right in front of them, they could have been seriously injured.

Silence is golden in golf. When someone is preparing for a shot, keep quiet, particularly on the putting green. When you are talking to one of your partners it is easy to forget that, although golf is a social sport, it is also an athletic game. Be considerate of those who are about to make their shots, and give them your full attention. Always watch where your partner's ball lands. This speeds up play and also develops a sense of partnership and camaraderie among players. The person who tees off first on a hole is the one who has the lowest score. This player has the honor, so make sure you keep track of your partner's score so you know when it is your turn to tee off. If you are not sure what her score is simply, ask.

A woman playing the red tees, who is playing with a group of men who hit the ball farther than she, might tee off first, regardless of who has the honor. Let's say you are a woman who hits your tee shot 175 yards, and the men in your group hit their tee shots about 220 yards. If you are on the tee waiting for a group that is 220 yards in front of you, you might say, "I can't reach them. Do you mind if I hit?" It is a waste of time for you to stand there waiting for your turn simply because you do not have the honor. However, if you are not delaying the group behind you, be respectful by letting the player who has the honor to hit first, unless, of course, he suggests that you go ahead. Some people are slower to get out of their carts and prepare themselves for a shot. So not always does the individual with the honor want to hit first. He might say, "Let's play 'ready golf.' If you're ready, go ahead and hit." There is nothing wrong with this as long as it is agreed upon by all members of the foursome.

When you think that your shot might hit another player, yell, "Fore!" A golf ball is very dangerous when traveling at a high speed. And likewise, if you hear anyone scream, "Fore," immediately crouch and cover your face and temples with your arms. If for any reason you hit a shot into the foursome in front of you, immediately go to them and apologize. If anyone ever intentionally hits a ball into your group, regardless of his reasoning, you have my permission to impale them with your pitching wedge. Not only is intentionally hitting a ball into a group extremely rude, but it is also very dangerous. Please make sure you report the offender to the pro shop after your round. People who do such acts should not be welcome on golf courses.

Upon starting a round of golf, if you are going to be driving the cart, place your golf bag directly behind you on the driver's side. Always be careful when starting the cart to make sure it is in forward gear. If, when you start the cart, you hear a prolonged beep, that means you have it in reverse. Do not put your foot all the way down on the accelerator until you're sure that all systems are go. I have seen golfers hop into a cart, ready to go to the first hole and slam their foot on the accelerator, only to go backward into another foursome. Golf carts can be dangerous, so drive them as if you were driving a car. Keep your feet inside the cart while it is moving. When you are anticipating getting to your ball, it is easy to hang a leg out without realizing it. Be careful because spikes caught in the ground or a leg pinched against a tree can be pretty uncomfortable. When you see a sign that says "Keep Carts on Cart Path," do just that. A golf cart driving on a soggy fairway can do terrible damage to a course. Leaving the cart on the path and walking to your ball isn't going to kill you. Take several clubs with you so you do not have to walk all the way back to the cart if you have the wrong club.

When driving the cart, do not get closer than 20 yards to the green and 10 yards to the sand traps. Always position the cart so it is ready to go to the next hole at the farthest end of the green. After you finish a hole, do not sit in the cart and tally your score. You are a distraction to the players behind, who are waiting to hit to the green, and you are in a dangerous position to be hit. When you complete a hole, immediately drive to the next tee and tally your score there. When you take a practice swing, always take it while standing in the rough because if everyone took a practice swing in the fairway (and with it, a divot), golf courses would start looking pretty shabby. Particularly if you are in the teeing area, just step off to the side where the long grass is and take several practice swings. Then approach your ball to make your shot. When you show respect for a golf course you show respect for the game, the other players, and yourself.

If you are a beginner, you should always let the people you are playing with know that you are new to the game. Inform them that you are not knowledgeable about golf etiquette and ask them to please correct you if you do something wrong. Always make sure the pro shop attendant knows that you are a beginner because often they know people who enjoy playing with beginners and will pair you with them. And ask questions if you do not understand something; that is the only way you will learn. It is much more enjoyable to play a round of golf with someone who is polite and congenial than it is with someone who hits a decent ball but is rude and scornful of etiquette. So you see, your golf swing is not always the most important factor in determining a pleasurable round of golf for both you and your partners.

Women Who Are New to Golf

Female newcomers to golf are often stunned by the bias against them in the golf world. In many parts of the country, golf clubs will not let women on the course on specific days. They are not even welcome in the pro shop or driving range on certain days. I know of one club that was hosting a U.S. Women's Open Qualifying Tournament in which I was supposed to play. The tournament was scheduled for Friday and due to my heavy work schedule, the only time I could take my practice round was on Wednesday, two days before the tournament. I called to arrange a tee time only to be told, "Sorry, we cannot let you on the course." I said that I would play late in the evening and that there would be no problem. The pro shop attendant then replied, "We do not let any women on the golf course on Wednesday—only men." That was one of the worst slaps in the face toward women that I have seen by a USGA. sanctioned event: to hold a top regional women's qualifying tournament and then two days before the tournament not permit women to play the course?

You will find similar attitudes at public golf courses. Some are just plain rude to women, letting them know that they are not welcome. Always remember you have paid your greens fees and you have just as much right as men to be on the golf course, if not more (since you are natural golfers). Those of you who are starting golf now, I hope that by the time you start playing with a higher level of proficiency, these attitudes will have started to change.

19

Observations on Women and Golf

It Amazes Me That Women Ever Learn to Play Golf!

When a woman registers for a lesson, the lesson will often be assigned to the staff's beginning teaching professional. If you are lucky, the inexperienced teaching professional (say, it's a man) will take pride in his job. Unfortunately, usually the opposite case is true. The new pro, wanting to be one of the guys, will grudgingly take the lesson, and if he has any expertise he is not going to waste it on a woman.

Sometimes female pros discriminate, too. However, if there is a female pro she will usually take the lesson, regardless of whether she is qualified to teach the student. I remember golf school that had a competent female professional and a less competent female pro on staff. The competent pro became very popular. Women loved to take lessons from her because she really improved their games. The male professionals apparently felt threatened by having a competent woman on the staff because they thought it was making them look bad. The staff made it as difficult as possible for this woman to teach. Whenever possible, one male professional would stand next to her when she was giving a lesson and try to talk louder than she to distract her and her student. The head pro and his staff treated her without respect although she did roughly twice as many lessons as they did and her students raved about her.

The less competent woman was treated differently. The male pros tried to push women requesting lessons in her direction because they said she was a good "girl's" teacher, and they were courteous to her. If you asked the male pros if the less competent professional had any expertise on the golf swing, they would say no, but it did not matter because she was just teaching "girls." Asked if the competent pro knew what she was talking about, they would say yes but it was unfair that she was making all that money. The idea of having a competent, popular, female teaching professional among a staff of four men was too much for them to handle.

This type of discrimination eventually hurts the female player. How is a woman ever going to improve if she cannot get competent instruction? Until recently golf was a game that wealthy older women were privileged to enjoy. The prevalent attitude toward women's participation in sports during the era in which most of these women were raised was that women should pursue sports only on a social level. And I am always amazed at how women who know nothing of any athletic motion can be so adept at hitting a golf ball. Most men in their lives have experienced team sports, such as baseball and football, and even if they are not coordinated, they have been instructed and trained in the basic knowledge of some form of athletic motion. Men participate in team sports in and out of school. The emphasis traditionally has been much stronger for men and also begins at a much younger age in the playing of baseball and football.

I must confess that when I started teaching golf I was biased; I never took female golfers seriously. Whenever I thought about good golf I always thought in terms of men. I somehow had it in my mind that all men were coordinated and most women were not. Boy, have my attitudes turned 360 degrees! The more I taught and watched men, the more I realized that although they were stronger, they were not necessarily more coordinated. And the more I watched the women the more I realized that despite their weaker upper body strength, their coordination was great!

On the subject of women's lack of upper body strength, I also firmly believe that golf clubs play a very important part in a woman's golf swing. For many years women's golf clubs were made with men's throw-away shafts. By this I mean that shafts that were really men's flexes that were faulty or not good enough to put into a man's club were put into a woman's club with the rationale that it wouldn't make any difference because women couldn't hit balls anyway. I also wonder about the design of golf clubs. When clubs were invented, they were invented with the expectation that a man would be swinging them rather than a woman. I wonder how the evolution of the clubmaking industry would be different if they were originally designed for a woman's game. With all these factors going against women, I sometimes wonder how women learn to play at all!

A prominent businesswoman who needed to learn to play golf for business reasons explained to me that she had paid quite a bit of money to attend a week-long golf school. During that week, she was taught the theory of the golf swing. She felt quite comfortable with the swing theory; however, she confessed that she had one problem. She could not hit the ball. I asked her what she meant. "Doesn't it go into the air? Do you hit it left or right?" She looked at me anxiously and replied, "I cannot hit the ball. I mean, I miss it completely. I need help!" She told me that she spent a whole week without ever hitting a golf ball because she could not make contact. She said she was terribly embarrassed by the experience and confessed that she had no athletic ability and little physical strength. She was just a beginner and had already spent over two thousand dollars on golf lessons.

I told her that in all my years of teaching I had never encountered a student whom I could not get to make contact with the ball within ten minutes. She looked at me and said, "All the pros I have been to have told me that I am not capable of hitting a ball. What you are saying is impossible." I said, "First I am going to have to deprogram you. Forget your two thousand dollars' worth of lessons and just do as I say. Within ten minutes she was hitting the ball into the air without a tee and, I might add, quite well. She was so excited about her new-found success that she begged me to give her a lesson the following day. I recommended that she wait three or four days and get a little practice before coming back.

When she returned she was a completely different woman. No more self-doubt: She was making contact with the ball regularly and remarked that several men had commented on what a nice swing she had. After about six lessons I saw her with a friend at the driving range. Believe it or not, she was telling her friend how to swing the club correctly and was actually giving her some good advice. Basically what had happened to this student was that her first teachers had given her lessons that had made the golf swing so complex that she was trying to control the club rather than just her swing. On top of that, they had intimated to her that women were not suited for the golf swing, which confused her and destroyed her self-confidence.

Whoever those golf professionals were, I would love for them to see her today. She hits a beautiful ball and absolutely loves playing golf. So you see how the story could have gone the other way. If she had not come to me, she would have continued thinking that as a woman she was not capable of playing golf and would have missed out on a lot of fun on the golf course. Now she has learned that being a woman makes her more capable of playing golf and she now has the knowledge and confidence that will help her to improve her game.

Women Just Don't Listen

I do not know how many times I have heard male golf professionals say women are difficult to teach because they just don't listen. When I started teaching golf, all the male professionals kept saying to me, "Wait until you start teaching some of these ladies; they don't listen to a thing that you say. They'll make you absolutely nuts!" At first, not knowing any better, I listened to this line of reasoning and thought that this was just another minus regarding the majority of women golfers: Not only could they not hit the ball, but they wouldn't listen when you tried to help them. Prepared for the worst, I was pleasantly surprised. I started to realize not only were my female students natural golfers, but they were also easy to teach. They seemed to grasp what I was saying easily and were very attentive, asking questions whenever they did not understand. I have to say in terms of listening and comprehension of the golf swing I would rank nearly all of them as tens.

Most of these women would say to me, "You know, that makes a lot of sense; no one has ever taken the time to explain that to me." I started to realize that it wasn't that women don't listen, it was just that no one had been explaining much to them. One of the other golf professionals where I worked constantly complained about the women he would teach. "They are just like my wife—they don't listen," he would say, shaking his head. I decided to listen to him give a woman a lesson to see what all the commotion was about.

His student was a normal middle-aged female with adequate ability, but I noticed that he was talking entirely differently to her than he would talk with men.

He would not let her question him. He was talking at her, not to her. He would describe some part of the swing and when she would try to ask a question he would say, "Wait until I am finished talking." Well, of course, the woman—not being able to ask anything when she couldn't comprehend what he was saying—completely lost his train of thought, so he ended up having to repeat things over and over. It wasn't that she didn't hear what he had to say; she did not understand it well enough to execute it properly. I also noticed he was much harsher with her than he would have been with a man. If she did not immediately do what he asked her to, he would roll his eyes in frustration. I later gave this same woman lessons and found her to be very understanding. I had to ask her to question me if she did not understand anything; however, in the course of the lesson there were very few questions. She seemed to comprehend all that I taught her.

As I got to know these male professionals I realized that they expected me to listen to their thoughts about swing theory much as a student. If I ever interjected a comment about my beliefs it was as though I were interrupting them. My opinions were not regarded, yet I was expected to sit and listen to them. And mind you, it would have been an easy task for me to beat the majority of them on any given day, playing a course from the same tees. It may be that men and women speak a different language, however, I tend to think not. I have taken lessons from and seen some excellent male professionals teach. And from what I have seen, the professional's attitude toward women has a strong influence on how he teaches them. It is simple logic that if you talk at and not to someone, you are going to lose their attention. And if you are short-tempered, they are never going to learn from you.

Here is another personal memory of poor male-to-female golf instruction. A group of forty women from a local college came to the club where I worked for a group lesson. The lessons were to meet once a week for six weeks and each would last one hour. The group was divided into two, with a male golf professional assigned to each group of twenty. I had watched these golf professionals give many group lessons before, but always to men, and I knew their styles well. I watched how these professionals changed the manner in which they normally taught, and how they adjusted for the fact that they were teaching women.

Normally when teaching a group you try to get students to participate as soon as possible so you do not lose their interest. You want them all swinging their clubs and hitting range balls so they not only learn but enjoy themselves. These pros started by talking, without fielding any questions, and then made the women watch them hit golf balls. By this point most of the women were getting fairly bored. Then the professionals made each woman come to the tee one at a time and swing the club in front of them and the rest of the group. What these pros were doing was trying to control and dominate this group. They didn't expect anyone to be able to learn very much. As I watched this going on I thought to myself, "Well, there are forty more women who will probably never learn to play golf after this experience." It turned out I was pretty much on target: The class which had started with forty, had less than twenty participating near the end of its session. I have seen this sort of thing happen often, and I find it very upsetting to think of how many thousands of female golfers turn away from the game purely because of some bad experiences with male pros. It really is a wonder that even with events like these, women are still the fastest growing segment of the golfing population. Let's hope it continues to grow.

Thinking about how so many women have been taught incorrectly brings to mind a story about a golf professional at a country club where I used to teach. Although I was well versed in the knowledge of the golf swing from having worked on my own game and having helped other professionals with theirs, this would be the first time that I had taught golf professionally. When I started working at this country club the head professional, Tom, commented on how nicely I hit the ball and how I didn't swing at all like a girl. At first I didn't quite know how to react. I had never thought of myself as swinging a club like a man and wasn't really flattered by the comment. I always thought of myself as a good female golfer. After Tom repeated this to me several times, I finally asked what exactly he was talking about. He then showed me on my backswing that the manner in which my wrists cocked was not normal for a "girl." "Most girls swing like this," he said, making a backswing where the back of the left wrist remained flat at the top of the swing. He then showed me the "guy's" wrist position, in which the back of the left hand is cupped. I thought to myself, "I have been swinging like this from day one, and I have seen other good female golfers play, and their wrists don't hinge like a 'girl's.'"

As I became popular at my new place of employment, many of the women who had taken lessons from the head professional were now asking for me. I remember the first time I gave one of his students a lesson. Mary was a woman in her sixties who was an excellent athlete and known for her ability to hit a long ball. Besides playing golf well, she was an avid and competent tennis player. She told me that she had seen me giving lessons and she thought perhaps taking a lesson from another woman might help her with her swing. When she swung the club back the first thing I noticed was that her wrists were in that "girl's" position at the top of her backswing. For a moment I thought maybe Tom was correct; perhaps this was a natural position for most women to assume. However, when I showed her the correct way her wrists should hinge, she said, "You know, the top of my backswing has always felt uncomfortable. I'll bet that is the reason why." I then asked why she had hinged her wrists in that manner to start with. She replied, "Because I thought that was what you were supposed to do. Tom told me to cock my wrists like this because I wasn't strong enough for them to hinge in the manner you are showing me."

As more of Tom students came to see me, I noticed that they all cocked their wrists in the same manner. Their explanation was always the same: Tom had told them to swing like this because they were not strong enough to swing the other way. I changed their wrist position at the top of their swing from what Tom had called a girl's position to his "man's" position. None of these women had any problem making the transition. If anything, they commented on how much easier and natural it felt.

What I feel had happened was that Tom had seen several women swinging in this manner and then had started teaching all his female students to do the same. He just got it into his head that that was the way "girls" should swing a golf club, and he perpetuated this myth by teaching all the women to swing in this manner.

I never brought up this subject to Tom. He knew he was in the wrong when he saw me changing their swings and watched these women improve as they never did before. The one I felt the worst for was Mary. After spending a lot of money on golf lessons from Tom and his assistants, her swing had been almost completely destroyed because this myth Tom had taught her had led to more swing problems. She had been told so much misinformation about her swing that it took a long time to straighten her out. I think that some of the information that she was given was done maliciously. The male pros, seeing her talent and how far she could hit the ball, did everything possible to keep her in her place and make sure she hit a ball like a "girl." Perhaps someone has described your own swing as "hitting that ball just like a guy." If so, by no means take this as a compliment. You are a woman, and you

GOLF IS A WOMAN'S GAME

hit the ball like a woman, and that ability should be expected and respected when playing a woman's game.

You Have Yet to See Our Best!

You have to realize that until recently golf was not a socially acceptable sport for a woman to pursue. As a matter of fact, sports in general were not socially accepted female pursuits. If you keep this in mind you will realize that if you take ten athletically talented boys and ten athletically talented girls, nine out of ten boys will most likely take up sports. However, with the girls, it will be surprising if four out of the ten take up a sport. So already you are working with one-quarter less the original talent.

Let's say that all the boys and girls take up golf. As they progress through the teenage years, they will be sidetracked with the discovery of the opposite sex. But for the boys, playing golf fulfills their male role as competitors so they will be encouraged to play. Whereas the girls, wanting to be accepted by the opposite sex and fearful of displaying strength and competency (unfeminine traits), are more likely to give up golf and pursue more socially acceptable female roles. So where you started with ten talented athletes, you will be fortunate if you wind up with two girls who pursue golf through their teens. With the boys, you probably will have eight out of the ten continuing their golf. This progression continues throughout life so that out of one hundred talented males who began golf as children, about half will probably pursue professional golf. However, with the women, out of one hundred talented child golfers you will be lucky if ten pursue golf professionally.

So the players on the LPGA tour are representative of about 10 percent of the talent that exists. Considering the small pool of talent available to draw from, it is amazing how competent the female professionals are and how far they can hit the ball. Right now, we are only seeing 10 percent of the potential talent that exists. Can you imagine how many more Laura Davieses are out there? Or perhaps women who can hit the ball even farther? *We have yet to see all our talent!*

Red, White, and Blue: The All-American Tees

Before a woman steps onto a golf course the bias exists. The course has already been divided into men's and women's by the red, white, and blue tees. The red tees are the "ladies'" tees, the shortest length of the course. The men's tees (white), are farther back, and the male professional tees (blue) are the longest distance. I think these distinctions are one of the most discriminating things done in golf. Attributing a sex to each tee has really confused the fluidity of a round of golf. Men who should be playing the red tees refuse to do so because those are considered the women's course and are playing the blue tees, trying to prove to others their superior male golfing prowess, which is nonexistent. The result is that such division slows play. Women are always getting blamed for being the slow players, but if you ask any ranger at a golf course which sex is slower, he will tell you that the men are. I have played golf in foursomes with three men, and if play is slow they will look around the course, point at some women, and say, "Those ladies are holding us up!" when in reality a slow foursome of men, not women, is to blame. It just seems that women have become scapegoats for the frustration men are feeling about their inadequate golf games.

On a social round of golf, I often find it very confusing having to decide which tees from which to play. I normally play from the white tees—the normal-length course—only it depends on the nature of the group with which I am playing. If I'm playing with another couple, it's likely that the man will feel he has to outdrive me on every shot, and if he is not a very good golfer this can lead to a long day on the golf course. He will inevitably put so much pressure on his swing to knock the ball out there that it will fall apart, leaving him and everyone playing with him miserable. So you see that the distinction between the markers can ruin a social round of golf.

I like courses that now have four or even five sets of tees. This has thrown off the conventional thinking of men's, women's, and professional male's tees. It gives the players a variety of distances to play, which is good. They are distinguished by color, i.e, gold, blue, red, white, green. It gives men who should not be playing the regular-length course a shorter course to play without losing face. It also gives women a faster round of golf because these men are no longer tying up the course!

Another positive aspect of the fourth tee is that women who hit a long ball now have the option of playing a course that is not as short as the red course and not quite as long as the white course. So it gives them a chance to test their game against a slightly longer course.

When people play golf, they often use the same clubs over and over again. For example, you may hit your driver and No. 5 iron all day long on the par 4s and become fairly proficient with the No. 5 iron. However, this can lead you to lack confidence when hitting with any other iron so that when you are invited to play a course shorter than your home course you may not score as well as usual because you haven't used your No. 7 iron in such a long time. I remember playing a 6400-yard course constantly for a while, and I played it quite well. The only problem was that I developed a game that emphasized long drives and good chipping and putting. You may wonder what was wrong with that. The problem was that when I pulled the No. 8 iron out of the bag, I didn't know how far it would hit the ball or in what direction the ball would go. So whenever I played a shorter course I would actually score higher.

You also have to remember that just because a course is shorter it does not mean that it is easier. Not only will it emphasize a different part of your game but the course layout can require more precise shots. The next time you play golf, take a look at each hole from the men's and women's tees. Depending on your course design, you should find a different angle of approach as well as a difference in distance. I strongly urge men and women to play the different tees; it will only strengthen their game.

Men and Women on the Golf Course

A story that best illustrates the relationship between men and women on the golf course is that of a husband and wife who played golf four times a week at a course where I was a pro shop attendant. All the female employees, myself included, fell in love with the man. He was charming and considerate—the epitome of a true gentleman. His wife was equally charming, and he worshiped her dearly. They had been married fifty years, and their marriage reflected true love and respect for one another. They were club members and would always play late in the afternoon—often with other members. Since they came in so late in the day and were well versed in etiquette, there was really no reason to monitor their actions on the golf course.

Every time they played they would purchase two separate golf carts. I always thought they did this in case they might see someone walking on the course and invite the golfer to ride along. One rainy morning when there were no other players on the course, I asked the wife why they wanted two carts. She replied, "My husband and I have been married for fifty years. We have been through much together, and I truly love and revere the man, but *damn him*! When we get on the course, all he does is tell me what to do! So I insist on two separate carts so we can play together without having him bother me!" This is probably why their relationship had lasted fifty years: They knew their strengths and weaknesses as a couple and realized that golf did not add to the strength factor. (By the way, she was much better at the game than he, yet he was always full of suggestions on ways for her to improve her game.)

I witnessed another example of male-female relations on the golf course once where a twosome of men was unknowingly paired with a twosome of women. The men, upon finding out that they had been paired with two women, insisted that they play separately from the women. This occurred on a very busy day, and it was not possible to send back-to-back twosomes onto the golf course. The golf professional said to the men, "What difference does it make? They might be better golfers than you." The men stuck to their guns and insisted that they play separately. Well, the starter watching all this happen turned to the women who had been politely waiting to tee off and said, "You ladies go first." With a backed-up tee line watching and after suffering much humiliation, these women proceeded to the red tees. They both hit beautiful drives right down the middle of the fairway. They moved along swiftly and hit their second shots on target again. The men now were next in line to tee off and they approached the tee. The first topped his ball, and it rolled almost to the red tees. The second hit an unbelievable slice that took him into the next fairway.

After hitting these two miserable shots, the men grumbled about how the women had upset them and said this was, of course, the reason that they had hit the ball so poorly. The starter who had watched it all shook his head as he pointed toward the men and said, "They're the ones that should be playing from the red tees. They'll never catch up to those ladies!"

Sometimes women come to me wanting to learn to play golf because they feel it will strengthen their relationship with the men in their lives. I just have to shake my head because I know that the odds of this are slim and next to none. As a matter of fact, I hope they have a solid relationship with their men before they step onto the course because chances are that improving their golf will put a strain on their relationship. As I have said before, I think most men have difficulty being beaten by women.

I have played golf with male friends who, upon losing, behaved absolutely monstrously about the "injustice" of the situation, often claiming that I cheated or hustled them and placing me in the role of the nefarious woman. I once played quite frequently with a man whom I beat on a regular basis. One day, after we had just completed a round of golf, I bumped into his girlfriend. Her first question was, "Did he win or lose?" I replied that he had lost. She looked anxiously at me and said, "He is always in such a terrible mood after you beat him." Then, smiling and giggling, she added, "But keep doing it. I'm in your corner!"

I once gave golf lessons to a very nice elderly woman who was a prominent member at a rather exclusive southern country club. She did not hit the ball very far, and her only goal was to get the ball to reach the fairway from the ladies' tees. However, she complained to me that the men were trying to make the course a man's course and, she felt they were trying to discourage any women from playing by making the course unfairly long. Apparently, for a drive to reach the fairway from the ladies' tee, it would have to travel 175 yards. This was not an easy feat for many of the women, particularly the elderly women at the club. After hearing her complain, I suggested that she approach the president of the men's association with the problem. She pondered that advice and then said, "That's not as easy as you may think. The men's association president is my husband." After a pause she added, "But believe me, he hears about it when we get home!"

Not long ago I was playing golf by myself, just enjoying the day and being content not to talk about golf to anyone for a few hours. I soon noticed that the only group in front of me was a foursome of men, who appeared to be playing very poorly and slowly. They were about four holes in front of me so I played slowly, hitting two balls or trying different shots since there was no one behind me. The fairways were side by side, so the men were aware of where I was hitting my ball. They were very nice, clapping or saying, "Nice drive", and "Gee, that was great." Finally one said, "When you catch up to us, please feel free to play through." I finally caught up to them on the eleventh tee. They were very polite and commented that I had a very nice swing.

With all four men watching me on the tee, I went over to my cart to select a club. The hole was uphill about 150 yards. As I pulled my club out of my bag and approached the tee, one of the men asked what club I was going to use. I replied "A No. 6 iron." He then looked at me and said, "Oh, no, honey, you need a No. 5 iron. This hole is longer than you think." Now here is a man who could not break one hundred telling me, whom he knows is a golf professional, what club to use! I said, "I think I will stick with what I have." As I was teeing the ball, another man said, "Aren't you teeing the ball a little high for an iron?" Trying to be polite, I replied, "No, this is the height I always tee the ball for an iron shot." He then said, "Try teeing it a little lower, and you'll hit the ball better." These were the same men who before were complimenting me on how well I hit the ball; now they were telling me how to hit the ball. All I could think of was, "Let me hit this ball and get the hell away from these guys."

I hit the ball. I did not catch it clean but I had the right club, and it landed about 5 feet below the hole. You would have thought I would have gotten some praise. But to the contrary: The man who had suggested I should tee the ball lower said, "If that tee had been a little lower in the ground, that ball would have been in the hole." Every time I have to play through a foursome of men I think to myself, "Just keep your cool." Because even though I can outdrive, outplay, and outscore them, they are always going to make some comments that are going to make them feel superior. I will admit that not all men are like this. As a matter of fact, some really appreciate a good swing made by a golfer, male or female. The only problem is that they are in the minority.

On another occasion, I had been invited to play golf with a foursome of women at a local semi-private club. It had rained very heavily the night before and we had been instructed to keep our carts on the path. These women were very conscientious players who respected the course and its rules. While we were playing, my group spotted some carts being driven onto the fairway of another hole. It was a foursome of men who clearly did not care about staying on the paths. At about that time one of the shop assistants came riding by and one of the women in my group pointed out the men's gross infraction. The attendant said he would go speak to them immediately. The woman I was riding with said, "That gets me so mad when they do that." I asked who the men were, and she replied, "They're our husbands, and they do that all the time!"

As a general rule I do not allow husbands to watch their wives take golf lessons because usually this puts a strain on both the wife and on me. The wife starts out saying, "It won't bother me if he watches," but if she is having a particularly bad day, where she is having trouble hitting the ball, it puts an added pressure on her to perform. I don't know how many times I have had wives say to me, "I promise he won't say a word during the lesson—he's not like that," and then ten minutes into the lesson the husband starts interjecting his theory on the golf swing. It wouldn't be so bad if some of these men knew what they were talking about, but most have a completely incorrect concept of the golf swing. Sometimes the most frustrating part of teaching women is that you know the husband will interfere. When I give a golf lesson, I put a lot of my energy into trying to make my student understand and execute what I am teaching. Nothing hurts more than seeing a student's husband approach her after a lesson, start telling her what is wrong, and advising her differently about her swing. I know right then and there that the half hour I just spent was completely wasted. A well-intentioned husband can mess up a good golf lesson in less than ten minutes! Ladies, as much as you would like your husband to help you with your swing, his advice might not be correct. Yes, he may be a good golfer, and I am sure he is not intentionally hurting your swing, but just try to let it go in one ear and out the other whenever he starts giving you advice.

Learning about Yourself and Others

One of the reasons I was so attracted to the game of golf is that it seemed very analogous to life. Since golf is such an individual sport, your successes are truly yours, although sometimes they are influenced by luck and sometimes your ability actually created this luck. Some days you play golf and nothing goes right—everything seems wrong. Even though you may be hitting the ball well, the rub of the green is against you. The fear of failure as well as the fear of success can make you miss a two-foot putt.

You learn a lot about people on the golf course. I have always felt that if you really want to get to know someone's personality, you should play several rounds of golf with him. A round of golf will take him through the whole gambit of human emotion. You will discover how he handles success and failure. You'll learn about his temperament and his ability to accept responsibility for his actions. For example, does he blame the course, the people he's playing with, or anyone else for his failures? When he wins, is he a good winner? Is it necessary for him to win to enjoy himself? How far will he go to win? Will he cheat if necessary? I have seen players cheat just for the sake of cheating. Even when not in trouble, they give themselves that extra edge by moving the ball illegally. If they are in the woods, they might take a swing and miss the ball, and claim it was a practice swing. They might even pretend they have found their lost ball by dropping a new one in its place.

These are all bits of information about a person's personality that are priceless. I refused to play golf in several benefit tournaments with a prominent politician because I knew he had a chronic problem with cheating. He cheated constantly and would throw a tantrum if he thought anyone might beat him. Needless to say, several years later he was caught in some political skullduggery and removed from office.

I also played golf with a minister, a respected man of the cloth, whom I caught cheating several times. I never could understand how he successfully found his ball every time I thought it went deep into the woods. I later found out that he had a hole in the right pocket of his loose-fitting shorts where he would put a ball, and when no one was looking he would drop the ball from his pocket onto the ground. He also had a nasty habit of marking his ball two inches closer to the hole than where it had landed. Several years later he left his church due to allegations that he had affairs with several female members of his congregation and that he had been involved in several unresolved financial matters. As I stated, both of these people were well regarded in the community, and I probably would have never noticed their propensity toward distrustful behavior had I not played golf seven or eight times with them. If you are honest with yourself, you will learn a lot about your own emotions. You might even find yourself doing some of the things that my dishonest partners engaged in.

Golf can be a precious opportunity for self-discovery. My feelings when making a 20 foot no-brainer putt were often the same as when I would enter a classroom unprepared for an exam: Just guess and hope you come close. Or when I knew I had played a good round of golf but just plain did not score well, I'd think: That's life; it happens. The golf course can be as unfair as life can often be; there are no certainties. Every time you set up to a new hole, it is a new game, the future of which has yet to be determined. Good golfers, like people in other fields who are successful in dealing with life, adapt well to change. If you want to play good golf, you cannot dwell on the past. If you make a nine on a par five, don't keep mentally repeating your mistakes stroke by stroke. Forget them and move on.

Golf as a Microcosm of Society

Although golf is just a game, we have seen how it can be analogous to life situations and tell us something about people. Another thing it can do is tell us about the attitudes and values of the society in which we live. Before I played golf I had never once thought of sexual discrimination. I always excused certain male behaviors as "guy things." After playing golf I began to realize that all those little "guy things" put together show an attitude of dislike toward women.

When I hear comments on the golf course like, "It's just a group of women—it doesn't matter," or "That's worse than a woman," or when I see clubs banning women outright from their premises on certain days, I know that this is not just golf. Golf is a symbol of a much deeper disease, and that disease is misogyny. Through this little game that we are playing, women are exposed to real-life bigotry every time they set foot on a golf course. And to trivialize it by saying it's just a "guy thing," as I once did, is a gross injustice to yourself. The attitudes on the golf course reflect the attitudes of society. We will have to watch for attitudes to change off the golf course before they happen on it.

Several years ago, when I was hitting some shag balls in an open field by a municipal golf course, I noticed some male golf team members from a local high school standing behind me, maybe 100 yards to my left. They began hitting golf balls, ignoring me even though I was in plain vision. This was not only rude of them but extremely dangerous for me. I heard one of the boys say, "Watch out, you might hit her." Another boy replied, "Who cares? It's a woman," and the boys, aged about fifteen, continued hitting.

I thought to myself what a sad state of affairs it is when someone risks another person's life without caring just because, in their eyes, she is "just a woman." I fear that when these boys grow older they will join a country club and maintain this same attitude. Their wives will probably dismiss their attitude as a guy thing, and think, "Golf is a silly game anyway—who really cares?" What they won't realize is that if their husbands have this attitude on the golf course, they will certainly carry it with them into the workplace and into their homes. And it will surface again and again.

Conclusion

I feel that the reason some men so dislike to see women playing golf is that we are a threat to them. Somewhere in the back of their minds men realize that women can beat them on the golf course, and I do not think they can handle that possibility. When I started playing golf fifteen years ago, I was told by golf professionals that as a woman I could not compress an iron shot anywhere equal to that of the average male golfer, who would always be two clubs stronger with his irons, hitting a No. 7 iron where I would hit a No. 5 iron. Well, fifteen years later I am hitting a No. 7 iron 150 yards, and I think you will find that this is two clubs stronger than your average male golfer!

Another factor that has greatly inhibited the progress of women in golf is the club-making industry. Until a few years ago, club makers ignored the female market. Where men had the luxury of choosing different shaft flexes and a wide range of quality clubs, women were left with clubs most of which had low-end men's flex shafts in them. How could a woman possibly expect to get distance with a club that had an inferior shaft in it? Fortunately, manufacturers are now coming out with clubs aimed at the women's market. Several companies offer shafts that come in three different flexes: stiff, medium, and flexible. A good quality club designed for a woman does make a difference. Every day I witness the results.

Although male-biased teaching methods are commonplace in golf, not all golf professionals are intentionally malicious in their teaching practices. Many pros are as much victims of misinformation as their students are. However, it is important to be aware that bias against women does exist and yet not to let it deter you. With the number of female golfers continuing to increase at its present rate, women will outnumber men playing golf by the year 2020!

Some myths that I have addressed in the book have been told to men as well as to women. Still, it has been my experience that women are the more likely targets of these tales, which are sometimes told maliciously. If you are a male reader, I hope that the next time you are on the golf course you will treat your female counterparts with the respect that they deserve. Please worry about your own game and do not tell a woman how she should swing the club. Most women have a naturally graceful swing and would not benefit from your advice.

It is my sincerest wish that this book will be of help to women who love golf but are frustrated in making progress with their game. Please, *never let anyone tell you that you are not physically designed to play golf. It is simply not true. As I hope this book has shown, women have a greater natural ability for golf than men.* So the next time you play golf and you hear a derogatory comment about female golfers, remember: *Golf is a woman's game.*

— *Jane Horn*

Appendix

Exercises

Right-Hand Full Swing Drill

Hitting balls with the right hand is an excellent exercise for right-handed golfers, designed to teach you not to throw the club head at the ball on the downswing. This also develops a sense of rhythm and timing and puts some feel into your swing. Since you are right-handed, it is important to train this hand not to dominate at the top of your backswing. To perform this drill simply take the club in the right hand with normal grip and stance and swing the club to the top of your backswing. Make sure you turn your shoulders as you would in a regular swing, and keep yourself tilted from the hips throughout the swing. The right wrist should hinge ninety degrees and be sure that it hinges vertically. Also, let the right arm bend at a ninety-degree angle forming the letter *L*. Once you are in this position, simply let the arm swing through on the same path as it did going back. Your finish should be in roughly the same position, only opposite that of your backswing. The primary items you want to concern yourself with on the backswing and follow-through are that the toe of the club should be pointing toward the sky when swinging back and when following through. Make sure that your hands move with the club head; do not let your wrists throw the head.

Right-hand full swing.

217

What makes this such a good exercise is that if you do throw the club head you will lose so much control that it is possible to hit yourself or take a large chunk of real estate on the downswing. You are not likely to do the former because of the subconscious need for self-preservation. The latter will jar your wrists, and again with self-preservation in mind, it is not something your body will let you do. Try every club from a pitching wedge to driver.

The Right-Hand Chip Shot

This is similar to the full swing exercise, only here you are going to take a small backswing (maybe two feet) and a small follow-through. This is great for giving you touch around the green. Also, if you are not confident about getting the ball in the air, this will give you that much needed boost. Once you see how little effort is necessary to loft a shot with just one hand, two hands on the club will seem like a piece of cake! The main idea for the execution of this shot is to have the hand move with the club head. Do not let the wrists swing the club.

The Right Hand Swings the Club, with the Left Hand Covering the Collarbone

This is ideal for getting the feeling of the proper upper body rotation. First, place your left hand over your collarbone toward your chest. Think of this as your center on your backswing. When your shoulders turn, this center will move so that the back of the left hand will be in a straight line with the right leg. On the follow-through, the back of the left hand will be in a straight line with your left leg. Do this in coordination with swinging the club with your right hand. You should feel as though the right arm is trying to catch up to your center. Do not let the center get too far ahead of the swinging right arm. At impact you should feel that your center and the right arm are in alignment (see illustration). This will help you get a feel for the upper body movement in relation to the arms and club. If your upper body gets too far ahead, this will cause you to hit behind or top the ball. Again, when you do this make sure that you keep the spine in the same tilted position it was in at address.

Swinging-Arms Drill

Do this exercise without a ball, and do it whenever you are loosening up before a round of golf or in between shots. First, set up in your normal address position. Then swing the club back and through and back and through, without stopping or accelerating in either direction. Do this motion nine or ten times, letting the club graze the grass. When you do this, you want minimum movement in your lower body—just the turning of the upper body and the swinging of the arms. If you feel that your lower body might be moving too much, put your feet completely together and repeat this exercise. This will help keep the lower body out of the swing.

Right hand swings the club while the left hand covers your center.

Let me describe the ball-hitting version of this drill. Place a ball on a tee about four feet in front of you. Now start this swinging motion. Slowly step closer and closer to the ball. When you finally get at a distance to hit the ball, go ahead and hit it. The important thing is not to stop swinging the club or not to direct it toward the ball. You simply want the ball to get into the way of the swinging club head. This is a great technique to learn rhythm and to keep from throwing the club head at the ball.

Press Forward Drill

This drill gives you the feel for the correct tempo of the backswing. Grip your club and hold it about hip-high, pointing in the direction of your target. Then let it swing to the top of your backswing. After a slight pause let it swing back through. The idea behind this exercise is that starting with the club in this position will give you enough momentum to have a faster and smoother back-swing.

This exercise can also be used to hit a ball. When the club goes swinging back, let it go over the top of the ball. And when it comes back down, simply let it make contact with the ball.

Start your swing from this position.

Left-Hand Full Swing Drill

This is similar to the right-hand drill, only with the left you can see how dramatically the arm leads on the downswing. If you are an average right-handed golfer, your left arm will be quite weak. This exercise will help increase the strength in your arm.

Two Hands Going Back, One Hand Coming Down Drill

For anyone whose left arm is very weak: Swing the club back with both the left and right hands. However, swing back down with only your left hand. This will give you the feeling of leading the downswing with your left arm and will also train your right arm to be more submissive when swinging through the shot.

Still Hips Drill

In this drill you try to keep the hips as still as possible on the backswing and downswing. Assume your address position and notice in what direction your left hipbone is pointing. On the backswing the hip is going to turn as your shoulders turn. When you execute the downswing, try to keep the left hip pointing in the same direction as at address for as long as possible. Do not let the hip slide out to the left. When making these shots, hit a No. 6 iron and use easy swings. If you have lower back problems or hip problems, you might want to hit only a few shots in this position and then make your regular swing.

The Claw Grip Drill

Grip the club with your left hand. Then, instead of placing the right hand on the shaft, place it on top of your left hand. Take some full swings. You will feel the left hand controlling the club. The right hand is positioned to give the left support, not to dominate. This is a good exercise for everyone, particularly those whose left arm is not strong enough to support the club on the backswing. This will strengthen the left arm and give you the feeling of your right hands' presence in the swing.

Full Swing with Feet Together

Put your feet together and, with both hands on the club, hit balls. This will teach you the proper upper body rotation as well as a sense of balance.

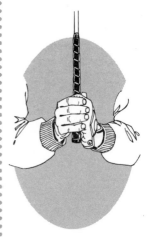

The claw grip.

Club Positioning at the Top of the Backswing

Stand erect and grip your club and point it straight from your body so that it is parallel to the ground. Now cock your wrists so the club is vertical to the ground. Turn your shoulders ninety degrees. Then raise your arms so the club is parallel with the ground. Bend from your hips thirty-five degrees. This is the top of your backswing. You might want to do this exercise in front of a mirror to reinforce your visual perception of this positioning.

Assume your address. Then cock your wrists ninety degrees vertically. Next turn your shoulders to the right. Raise your arms until the club is parallel or close to parallel. This is the club and hand position for the top of the backswing.

Blindfolded Drill

You don't actually have to be blindfolded to execute this drill; if you want, you can merely shut your eyes. Put a ball on a tee and make a few gentle swings. Then shut your eyes. It will be a very strange sensation at first. You might feel as though you have no control. As you become more familiar with this feeling you will relax, and it will not be as frightening. The purpose of this exercise is to make you lose the feeling of control. In other words, since you can no longer see the ball you will not feel the need to direct the club head directly at the ball. Instead, you will simply let the arms swing through. Do *not* swing hard or fast. Be sure to make a very gentle motion. Also, if you are uncomfortable with a full swing, make a shorter swing until you gradually reach the top of your swing.

Two-Person Drill

A good drill to get the feeling of the overall tempo and speed of the swing will require another person. Get in your address position, with the ball placed on a tee. Have a friend (say, it's a woman) stand facing you about a club's length away. She is going to hold a No. 3 iron by the club head. Once you are ready she is going to place her club so that the grip end is on the hosel of your club. You should be given a three count to get ready. Then she will swing your club back with just enough momentum for you to reach the top of your swing. Now let the club swing through and hit the ball. This is the rhythm of a good golf swing. Your friend has merely taken the weighted club head and set it in motion by swinging it back first. A word of caution to your friend: Make sure there is nothing behind or to the side of you. Once you set the club in motion, move backward toward the left, just in case of a shank. And to you who are swinging the club: Make sure you have a secure grip before your helper gets you started.

The Wall Drill

This is a good drill for anyone having a problem with a backswing that is too flat, or a roundhouse backswing. Stand against a wall. Then take one step forward. Set up in your normal address, then swing the club to the top of the backswing. It should not hit the wall. If it does, this means your hands or wrists are swinging around your body instead of moving vertically. Whenever you are at a practice range, imagine that wall behind you.

The Wall Drill for Wrist Angle

This drill is designed to teach you to cock your wrists by the time you reach the top of your backswing. It is also designed to teach you to maintain the wrist angle created by the cocking of your wrists on the downswing.

With your right side facing a wall, stand a No.6 iron's length away from the wall. Using your No.6 iron, assume your normal address. Now swing the club back and do not hit the wall with your club head.

The only way this can be done is for the wrists to start to cock as soon as the shoulders begin to turn. On your downswing let the arms swing through. Again, be careful not to hit the wall with the club head. This exercise will help you learn how not to throw the club head at the ball and help you maintain a cocked wrist position on your downswing.

Thumbs off the Club Drill

This is a great practice drill for getting the feel for the correct grip pressure. Grip the club as you normally would, only remove your thumbs and take several swings. Do this until you feel secure that you can hang on to the club and still hit a golf ball. Then start hitting very light and easy shots. *Be sure you hang on to the club!* Another great practice technique for someone who is very right-side dominant is to lift the thumb of your right hand off the shaft of the club and hit balls. For those of you who have trouble hanging on to the club with both thumbs removed, this is a safe way to practice. Also, with just your right thumb off the shaft you should be able to make your normal full swing without fear of the club's slipping out of your hands.

Putting Drills

To Improve Your Touch Around the Greens

One-handed putting exercises are an excellent way to improve your feel (touch) for the putting stroke. Simply hold the club in your left or right hand and putt the ball toward the hole.

Another great way to improve your touch is to hold the ball in your right or left hand, gently lob it into the air, and watch the ball roll toward the hole. By throwing the ball you are making your arm the shaft of the club and your hand the club face.

Experiment with different tosses. For example, try rolling the ball on the ground and then lob the ball into

Swing the club with the thumbs removed from the shaft.

the air. It is a great exercise and an enjoyable way to improve your putting.

Make putts by hitting the ball with different parts of the putter. For example, make a couple of putts by hitting the ball in the center (the sweet spot). Then hit a few by striking the ball closer to the toe. Finally make a few putts by striking the ball more toward the heel. This exercise gives you a better feel for your putter and for the putt.

Practice Putting Distances

Place a ball 2 feet from the cup. Place six more balls at 2-foot increments directly behind the first ball. Now, go to the first ball and putt it into the hole. Move to the second ball and do the same. Continue down the line until you have knocked all the balls into the hole. If you miss a putt at any point, try once more from the same spot; then continue on.

Do the same exercise, only place the balls 4 feet apart. First putt the ball into the hole. Now from the same spot while holding the ball, roll the ball to the hole. Do this until you have used all the balls. Again, if you should miss at any point, try once more and then continue on.

For putting long distances, pick a spot about three-quarters of the way to the hole; putt the ball firmly to this point; and let the ball drift the rest of the way to the hole. This drill teaches you on long putts to get the ball near or past the hole. This can be done by hitting it firmly and letting it trickle the rest of the way to the hole.

Putting Alignment

This exercise can be done in your home. Position four different targets that will require as many different body positions. For example, set one target so you are facing left, then straight, right, and a little farther right. Let's start with the target that is facing toward the left. Place two rulers (or anything similar to a ruler) parallel with each other 2^1/$_2$" apart. Now align the rulers so the chute (the 2^1/$_2$ inches) is pointed straight toward your target (a cup turned on its side). Place a ball in this chute. Now approach the ball from the rear. Treat this putt just as you would if you were on the golf course. Set yourself up and make the putt. Do this in all four different positions and do it from different distances. This is to train your eye to be able to see a straight line and set your body up accordingly.

Practice the Forward Stroke

When you make a putt, think of the back of the left hand as leading toward your target. On the backstroke, grip the putter with both hands. On the forward stroke, let go with your right hand and allow the left hand to stroke through by itself. This will teach you to stroke through the ball, as opposed to stopping at impact.

Aim for the back of the cup, not the front. This will encourage you to follow through.

Always picture how far you want to swing through on your forward stroke. This, of course, is based on the amount of backstroke you take.

Place a ball on a green. Then take a tee and place it 6 inches directly behind the ball. Now take another tee and place it 6 inches in front of the ball and off to the side so the ball will not hit it as it rolls to the hole. Make sure the club head reaches the tee on the backstroke and the forward stroke.

Index